Standards-Based
Math

Grades 5–6

by
Rebecca Waske

Published by Instructional Fair
an imprint of
Frank Schaffer Publications®

Instructional Fair

Author: Rebecca Waske
Editors: Sara Bierling, Chris Kjaer, Jeanine Manfro
Cover Artist: Jeff Van Kanagan
Interior Designer: Tracy L. Wesorick
Interior Artist: Jack Snider

Frank Schaffer Publications®

Instructional Fair is an imprint of Frank Schaffer Publications.

Send all inquiries to:
Frank Schaffer Publications
3195 Wilson Drive NW
Grand Rapids, Michigan 49534

Standards-Based Math—grades 5–6

ISBN: 0-7424-0216-9

8 9 10 11 12 13 14 MAZ 12 11 10 09 08 07

Introduction

Standards-Based Math is based on the most recent standards from the National Council of Teachers of Mathematics. The ten proposed NCTM standards, which are a description of what an existing curriculum should enable students to know and do, can be divided into two categories. The Content standards are those five that state the skill areas that students should learn. These are Number and Operations, Algebra, Geometry, Measurement, and Data Analysis and Probability. The Process standards, which guide instructors in planning lessons that enable students to acquire knowledge and achieve success, are the second set of standards. These standards are Problem Solving, Reasoning and Proof, Communication, Connections, and Representation.

For the purpose of this book, the Content standards have been highlighted, and each page is labeled with its appropriate standard and skill. The Process standards are woven into the exercises on each page.

The following are simplified descriptions of the Content standards.

Number and Operations
1. Understands numbers, number representation, relationships, and systems
2. Comprehends operations and their relatedness
3. Fluent in computation and estimation

Algebra
1. Recognizes relationships, functions, and patterns in numbers
2. Uses algebraic symbols
3. Shows similarities in math equations using models
4. Recognizes and evaluates change

Geometry
1. Has knowledge of two- and three-dimensional objects
2. Uses coordinate geometry
3. Recognizes symmetry and transformation
4. Solves problems using geometry

Measurement
1. Understands measurement
2. Uses a variety of methods to show measurement

Data Analysis and Probability
1. Understands the necessity of data
2. Utilizes statistics
3. Makes inferences and predictions based on data
4. Comprehends the basic principles of probability

Table of Contents

Geometry

Measurement

Data Analysis and Probability

Name _____

What's My Place?

Think about the placement of each digit below to answer the questions.

1. What number of 6,719 is in the hundreds place? _____

2. What number of 1,893 is in the tens place? _____

3. What number of 14,503 is in the ones place? _____

4. What number of 836,703 is in the hundred thousands place? _____

5. What number of 53,217 is in the ten thousands place? _____

6. What number of 6,392,540 is in the millions place? _____

7. What number of 4,974 is in the thousands place? _____

8. What number of 103,792 is in the thousands place? _____

Match each underlined digit in the decimal with its word form.

9.   4.802<u>4</u>

10.   204.<u>9</u>8

11.   0.0600<u>3</u>

12.   0.1<u>0</u>

a. zero hundredths

b. four ten thousandths

c. three hundred thousandths

d. nine tenths

Read the data below. Answer the questions.

13. This number has 4 places to the right of the decimal point. It has 2 hundreds, 3 ten thousandths, and 1 tenth. It is in between 240 and 242. The thousandths place is one less than the ten thousandths and less than the hundredths. What are six numbers that match this data?

_____
_____
_____
_____
_____

14. This number has a 0 in the ones place. The fifth digit to the right of the decimal sign is less than the first. The number in the thousandths place is the smallest number. The number in the ten thousandths place is half the value of the number in the hundredths place. This decimal contains a 4, 2, 1, 3, and 5. What is the number?

_____

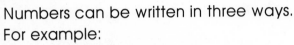

Don't Bug Me

Numbers can be written in three ways.
For example:

standard form = 465

expanded form = 400 + 60 + 5

word form = four hundred sixty-five

Study the chart and answer the questions.

Number of People Who Dislike Bugs

Spider	31,389,250
Centipede	14,003,632
Silverfish	752,430
Ant	30,621
Earwig	20,732,806
Beetle	5,885,761

1. In word form, how many people dislike ants? _____
_____

2. In expanded form, how many people dislike spiders? _____
_____

3. What is the total number of people who dislike earwigs and beetles? Write in standard form. _____

4. What bug's amount is 10,000 times 3,138.925? _____

5. Which two bugs' amounts each have a 3 in the ten thousands place? _____
_____

6. Write the total number of pieces of data in standard, expanded, and word form. _____
_____
_____
_____

Break It Down

Break down each whole number. Write in expanded form. Put back together to check your answer.

1. 11,763 _____

2. 9,651 _____

3. 25,341 _____

4. 742 _____

5. 2,962 _____

Compose each number into standard form.

6. 30,000 + 2,000 + 900 + 50 _____

7. 10,000 + 1,000 + 100 + 10 + 1 _____

8. 6,000 + 400 + 90 + 9 _____

9. 500 + 50 + 8 _____

10. 8,000 + 100 + 80 + 6 _____

Write the following amounts in words.

11. 23,042,368 _____

_____

12. 48,000,002 _____

_____

13. 2,000,500,000 _____

_____

14. 402,000 x 10 _____

_____

Name _____

Lines of Integers

Add the positive and negative integers. Illustrate your answer on the number line. The first one has been done for you.

1. 5 + ⁻7 = __-2__

2. 4 + ⁻3 = ____

3. 2 + ⁻6 = ____

4. 3 + ⁻5 = ____

5. 7 + ⁻6 = ____

6. 5 + ⁻2 = ____

7. ⁻6 + ⁻3 = ____

8. 10 + ⁻8 = ____

9. 9 + ⁻6 = ____

10. ⁻5 + ⁻2 = ____

Interesting Integers

Subtract the positive and negative integers. Remember, turn the subtraction problem into an addition problem and change the sign of the second number.

Example: 4 − ⁻8 = 4 + 8 = 12

1. 25 − ⁻16 = _____

2. ⁻118 − ⁻53 = _____

3. ⁻210 − 51 = _____

4. ⁻118 − 53 = _____

5. 44 − ⁻37 = _____

6. ⁻99 − ⁻42 = _____

7. ⁻62 − 3 = _____

8. 42 − 12 = _____

9. ⁻17 − ⁻5 = _____

10. ⁻86 − 42 = _____

11. ⁻10 − ⁻9 = _____

12. ⁻36 − ⁻15 = _____

13. 33 − ⁻14 = _____

14. ⁻36 − 15 = _____

15. 52 − ⁻7 = _____

16. 109 − ⁻35 = _____

Find each missing integer.

17. 1 − ⁻1 = 1 + ☐

18. ⁻2 − 5 = ⁻2 + ☐

19. 14 − ⁻5 = 7 + ☐

20. ⁻9 − ⁻6 = ⁻3 + ☐

21. 24 − 9 = ⁻9 + ☐

22. ⁻96 + ⁻13 = ☐ − ⁻18

Name _____

Integer Concept Review

Solve.

1. 12 + ⁻10 = _____

2. 46 + ⁻17 = _____

3. ⁻5 + 12 = _____

4. ⁻11 + 33 = _____

5. ⁻23 + ⁻30 = _____

6. 109 + ⁻59 = _____

7. 10 + ⁻27 = _____

8. ⁻37 – ⁻23 = _____

9. 28 – 19 = _____

10. 46 – ⁻17 = _____

11. ⁻65 – ⁻14 = _____

12. 59 – 12 = _____

Write the coordinates for each point below.

A = _____   B = _____   C = _____   D = _____   E = _____
F = _____   G = _____   H = _____   I = _____   J = _____
K = _____   L = _____   M = _____   N = _____

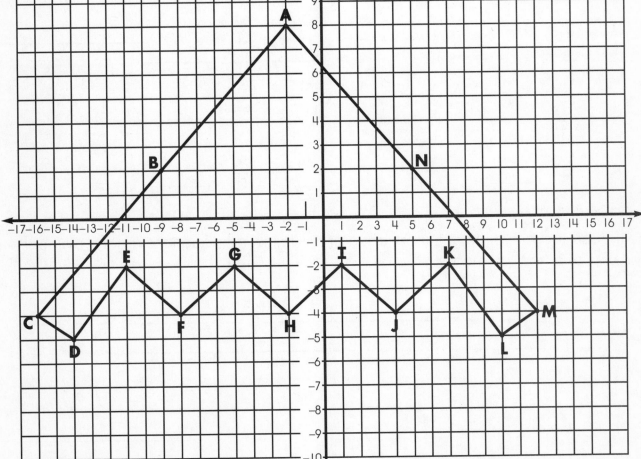

Let's Compare

Write in the correct sign for each problem: **<**, **>**, or **=**.

1. $\dfrac{8}{24}$ _____ $\dfrac{1}{3}$ 2. $\dfrac{30}{90}$ _____ $\dfrac{1}{6}$

3. $\dfrac{2}{6}$ _____ $\dfrac{1}{2}$ 4. $\dfrac{4}{124}$ _____ 1

5. $\dfrac{4}{8}$ _____ $\dfrac{1}{4}$ 6. $\dfrac{9}{27}$ _____ $\dfrac{1}{3}$

7. $\dfrac{6}{24}$ _____ $\dfrac{1}{4}$ 8. $\dfrac{9}{36}$ _____ $\dfrac{1}{4}$

9. $\dfrac{5}{10}$ _____ $\dfrac{1}{2}$ 10. $\dfrac{16}{32}$ _____ $\dfrac{1}{5}$

11. $\dfrac{5}{25}$ _____ $\dfrac{1}{10}$ 12. $\dfrac{3}{15}$ _____ $\dfrac{1}{5}$

13. $\dfrac{3}{9}$ _____ 1 14. $\dfrac{25}{150}$ _____ $\dfrac{1}{4}$

15. $\dfrac{3}{27}$ _____ $\dfrac{3}{4}$ 16. $\dfrac{25}{150}$ _____ $\dfrac{1}{6}$

Write one reason you might know each of the following equations are true without looking at a fraction model.

17. $\dfrac{7}{8} > \dfrac{2}{3}$ _____

_____

18. $\dfrac{3}{4} < \dfrac{9}{11}$ _____

_____

Name _____

Equal Time

Shade in all boxes with equivalent fractions to find the hidden fraction. Write it on the blank below and answer the question.

Is this statement true? _____ $= \frac{3}{5}$ Yes or No?

$\frac{14}{18} = \frac{7}{9}$	$\frac{20}{24} = \frac{5}{6}$	$\frac{5}{20} = \frac{1}{4}$	$\frac{4}{36} = \frac{1}{13}$	$\frac{4}{22} = \frac{2}{11}$	$\frac{12}{15} = \frac{4}{5}$	$\frac{18}{21} = \frac{6}{7}$
$\frac{20}{40} = \frac{1}{4}$	$\frac{13}{26} = \frac{1}{3}$	$\frac{3}{24} = \frac{1}{8}$	$\frac{3}{10} = \frac{1}{5}$	$\frac{4}{30} = \frac{2}{15}$	$\frac{35}{55} = \frac{7}{12}$	$\frac{10}{15} = \frac{2}{7}$
$\frac{10}{50} = \frac{1}{4}$	$\frac{10}{24} = \frac{5}{12}$	$\frac{6}{33} = \frac{2}{11}$	$\frac{4}{18} = \frac{2}{8}$	$\frac{14}{21} = \frac{2}{3}$	$\frac{6}{14} = \frac{3}{7}$	$\frac{20}{36} = \frac{5}{9}$
$\frac{3}{16} = \frac{1}{5}$	$\frac{8}{24} = \frac{1}{4}$	$\frac{8}{30} = \frac{4}{15}$	$\frac{16}{22} = \frac{6}{11}$	$\frac{12}{30} = \frac{2}{5}$	$\frac{8}{20} = \frac{1}{3}$	$\frac{3}{24} = \frac{1}{8}$
$\frac{5}{10} = \frac{1}{2}$	$\frac{10}{20} = \frac{1}{2}$	$\frac{14}{50} = \frac{7}{25}$	$\frac{14}{28} = \frac{2}{7}$	$\frac{6}{18} = \frac{1}{3}$	$\frac{6}{21} = \frac{2}{7}$	$\frac{10}{24} = \frac{5}{12}$
$\frac{20}{42} = \frac{1}{2}$	$\frac{14}{38} = \frac{1}{2}$	$\frac{26}{52} = \frac{13}{25}$	$\frac{12}{34} = \frac{1}{3}$	$\frac{15}{30} = \frac{1}{6}$	$\frac{16}{32} = \frac{1}{3}$	$\frac{8}{36} = \frac{2}{7}$
$\frac{4}{16} = \frac{1}{4}$	$\frac{2}{60} = \frac{1}{30}$	$\frac{20}{45} = \frac{4}{9}$	$\frac{6}{30} = \frac{1}{5}$	$\frac{10}{26} = \frac{5}{13}$	$\frac{25}{55} = \frac{5}{11}$	$\frac{6}{12} = \frac{1}{2}$
$\frac{27}{38} = \frac{9}{16}$	$\frac{75}{100} = \frac{1}{2}$	$\frac{18}{36} = \frac{9}{14}$	$\frac{17}{34} = \frac{1}{18}$	$\frac{50}{125} = \frac{2}{75}$	$\frac{4}{9} = \frac{2}{3}$	$\frac{18}{26} = \frac{9}{14}$
$\frac{6}{28} = \frac{3}{14}$	$\frac{4}{6} = \frac{2}{3}$	$\frac{6}{9} = \frac{2}{3}$	$\frac{3}{10} = \frac{1}{5}$	$\frac{12}{14} = \frac{6}{7}$	$\frac{10}{36} = \frac{5}{18}$	$\frac{4}{8} = \frac{1}{2}$
$\frac{12}{18} = \frac{2}{3}$	$\frac{14}{54} = \frac{7}{24}$	$\frac{13}{49} = \frac{3}{17}$	$\frac{24}{25} = \frac{4}{5}$	$\frac{35}{50} = \frac{7}{10}$	$\frac{35}{50} = \frac{8}{10}$	$\frac{2}{40} = \frac{1}{20}$
$\frac{25}{50} = \frac{1}{2}$	$\frac{16}{20} = \frac{4}{5}$	$\frac{10}{20} = \frac{1}{2}$	$\frac{9}{11} = \frac{3}{9}$	$\frac{9}{15} = \frac{3}{5}$	$\frac{28}{56} = \frac{7}{12}$	$\frac{11}{33} = \frac{1}{3}$
$\frac{10}{26} = \frac{5}{13}$	$\frac{17}{34} = \frac{1}{17}$	$\frac{3}{30} = \frac{1}{10}$	$\frac{4}{20} = \frac{1}{4}$	$\frac{11}{66} = \frac{1}{6}$	$\frac{4}{20} = \frac{1}{6}$	$\frac{4}{40} = \frac{1}{10}$
$\frac{21}{24} = \frac{7}{8}$	$\frac{25}{75} = \frac{1}{3}$	$\frac{22}{40} = \frac{11}{20}$	$\frac{3}{30} = \frac{1}{3}$	$\frac{40}{50} = \frac{4}{5}$	$\frac{22}{55} = \frac{2}{5}$	$\frac{9}{12} = \frac{3}{4}$

Name _____

We're Equal

Draw a line from each fraction on the left to its equivalent fraction on the right.

1. $\dfrac{25}{65}$

2. $\dfrac{18}{42}$

3. $\dfrac{25}{100}$

4. $\dfrac{20}{76}$

5. $\dfrac{36}{54}$

6. $\dfrac{24}{136}$

7. $\dfrac{7}{98}$

8. $\dfrac{21}{77}$

$\dfrac{3}{17}$

$\dfrac{3}{11}$

$\dfrac{1}{4}$

$\dfrac{3}{7}$

$\dfrac{5}{19}$

$\dfrac{5}{13}$

$\dfrac{2}{3}$

$\dfrac{1}{14}$

Write the missing numerator or denominator.

9. $\dfrac{4}{} = \dfrac{20}{35}$

10. $\dfrac{}{8} = \dfrac{49}{56}$

11. $\dfrac{18}{} = \dfrac{9}{16}$

12. $\dfrac{10}{15} = \dfrac{2}{}$

13. $\dfrac{2}{9} = \dfrac{}{63}$

14. $\dfrac{3}{5} = \dfrac{}{25}$

Parts and Wholes

Change each improper fraction to a mixed number. Circle the improper fraction that is a whole number.

1. $\frac{41}{3}$ _____

2. $\frac{55}{31}$ _____

3. $\frac{26}{19}$ _____

4. $\frac{121}{9}$ _____

5. $\frac{26}{25}$ _____

6. $\frac{113}{6}$ _____

7. $\frac{37}{8}$ _____

8. $\frac{93}{2}$ _____

9. $\frac{217}{217}$ _____

10. $\frac{64}{3}$ _____

Look at each fraction model. Write each as an improper fraction and a mixed number.

11.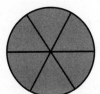

12.

13.

_____   _____   _____

Name _____

Working

The time clock at Burgerama tracks hours worked in improper fractions. Draw a line from each fraction to the correct mixed number to find out how long each employee worked.

1. $\frac{45}{13}$

2. $\frac{12}{5}$

3. $\frac{23}{4}$

4. $\frac{33}{5}$

5. $\frac{71}{2}$

6. $\frac{31}{7}$

7. $\frac{59}{6}$

8. $\frac{44}{6}$

9. $\frac{47}{4}$

10. $\frac{62}{9}$

$2\frac{2}{5}$

$4\frac{3}{7}$

$6\frac{3}{5}$

$35\frac{1}{2}$

$9\frac{5}{6}$

$11\frac{3}{4}$

$6\frac{8}{9}$

$7\frac{1}{3}$

$3\frac{6}{13}$

$5\frac{3}{4}$

11. Each hamburger at Burgerama weighs $\frac{1}{4}$ pound. If Sara started out with $7\frac{3}{4}$ pounds of hamburger, how many $\frac{1}{4}$ pound burgers could she make?

_____

12. If each breakfast pizza uses $\frac{1}{2}$ a muffin, and Leah needs to make 60 pizzas, how many boxes of muffins must be ordered if each box contains 15 muffins?

_____

Finding Sums

Find the common denominator, add the fractions, and reduce to lowest terms.

1. $\dfrac{5}{6} + \dfrac{1}{2} + \dfrac{2}{3} =$ _____

2. $\dfrac{4}{9} + \dfrac{2}{3} =$ _____

3. $\dfrac{3}{8} + \dfrac{2}{3} =$ _____

4. $\dfrac{2}{7} + \dfrac{1}{6} =$ _____

5. $\dfrac{7}{10} + \dfrac{2}{3} =$ _____

6. $\dfrac{2}{3} + \dfrac{1}{5} =$ _____

7. $\dfrac{2}{4} + \dfrac{2}{8} =$ _____

8. $\dfrac{3}{10} + \dfrac{5}{8} =$ _____

9. $\dfrac{3}{5} + \dfrac{3}{8} =$ _____

10. $\dfrac{3}{5} + \dfrac{1}{3} =$ _____

11. $\dfrac{1}{6} + \dfrac{1}{5} =$ _____

12. $\dfrac{3}{8} + \dfrac{1}{4} + \dfrac{5}{6} =$ _____

Name _____

Follow the Path

Add the fractions and fill in the blanks. Reduce each answer to lowest terms.

$\frac{1}{3}$	$+$	$\frac{4}{6}$	$=$	
$+$				
$\frac{5}{9}$	$+$	$\frac{3}{18}$	$=$	
$=$		$+$		
	$+$	$\frac{1}{6}$	$=$	
		$=$		
$\frac{3}{5}$	$+$		$=$	
$+$				
$\frac{7}{8}$	$+$	$\frac{9}{16}$	$=$	
$=$		$+$		
	$+$	$\frac{2}{8}$	$=$	
		$=$		

What's the Difference?

Find the common denominator. Subtract the fractions. Reduce to lowest terms.

1. $\dfrac{5}{8} - \dfrac{1}{2} =$ _____

2. $\dfrac{4}{11} - \dfrac{2}{9} =$ _____

3. $\dfrac{4}{9} - \dfrac{1}{3} =$ _____

4. $\dfrac{6}{7} - \dfrac{2}{5} =$ _____

5. $\dfrac{4}{7} - \dfrac{5}{9} =$ _____

6. $\dfrac{8}{9} - \dfrac{3}{4} =$ _____

7. $\dfrac{7}{8} - \dfrac{1}{4} =$ _____

8. $\dfrac{5}{12} - \dfrac{1}{9} =$ _____

9. $\dfrac{5}{6} - \dfrac{4}{5} =$ _____

10. $\dfrac{8}{9} - \dfrac{2}{3} =$ _____

11. $\dfrac{9}{10} - \dfrac{1}{6} =$ _____

12. $\dfrac{4}{5} - \dfrac{7}{10} =$ _____

List the fractions from least to greatest. Find the sum and the difference of the least and the greatest.

13. $\dfrac{3}{8}, \dfrac{1}{4}, \dfrac{5}{12}$ _____

14. $\dfrac{4}{5}, \dfrac{3}{10}, \dfrac{7}{8}, \dfrac{3}{4}$ _____

Name _____

Seawater Solutions

Subtract and reduce each answer. Then place the corresponding letter of each answer on the line below to solve the riddle.

1. $\dfrac{21}{25} - \dfrac{11}{25} =$ _____

2. $\dfrac{17}{30} - \dfrac{8}{30} =$ _____

3. $\dfrac{20}{24} - \dfrac{12}{24} =$ _____

4. $\dfrac{5}{20} - \dfrac{1}{20} =$ _____

5. $\dfrac{27}{40} - \dfrac{9}{40} =$ _____

6. $\dfrac{51}{100} - \dfrac{41}{100} =$ _____

7. $\dfrac{66}{100} - \dfrac{16}{100} =$ _____

8. $\dfrac{33}{99} - \dfrac{3}{99} =$ _____

| $\frac{1}{10}$ = E | $\frac{2}{5}$ = K | $\frac{1}{3}$ = L | $\frac{1}{5}$ = C | $\frac{10}{33}$ = P | $\frac{3}{10}$ = O | $\frac{9}{20}$ = Y | $\frac{1}{2}$ = M |

What is green and as large as a whale?

$\overline{}_7$ $\overline{}_2$ $\overset{\textbf{B}}{\overline{}}_5$ $\overline{}_8$ $\overset{\textbf{I}}{\overline{}}_4$ $\overline{}_1$ $\overline{}_3$ $\overline{}_6$

Find each missing fraction.

9. $\dfrac{17}{19} - \underline{} = \dfrac{3}{19}$

10. $\underline{} - \dfrac{3}{8} = \dfrac{2}{8}$

11. $\underline{} - \dfrac{11}{30} = 1$

12. $\dfrac{19}{25} - \underline{} = \dfrac{6}{25}$

13. Five-sixteenths of an aquarium holds lobsters; $\dfrac{7}{16}$ holds crabs. What fraction of the aquarium is left for clams? _____

14. A fish tank holds 30 fish. One-sixth of the fish are guppies. What fraction of the fish are not guppies? _____

Name _____

Cycling for Fractions

Aren is making deliveries on his bike. He follows his boss's directions and zigzags across downtown. To find out how many miles Aren went in all, add fractions under **GO** signs and subtract fractions under **STOP** signs. Write each answer on the line.

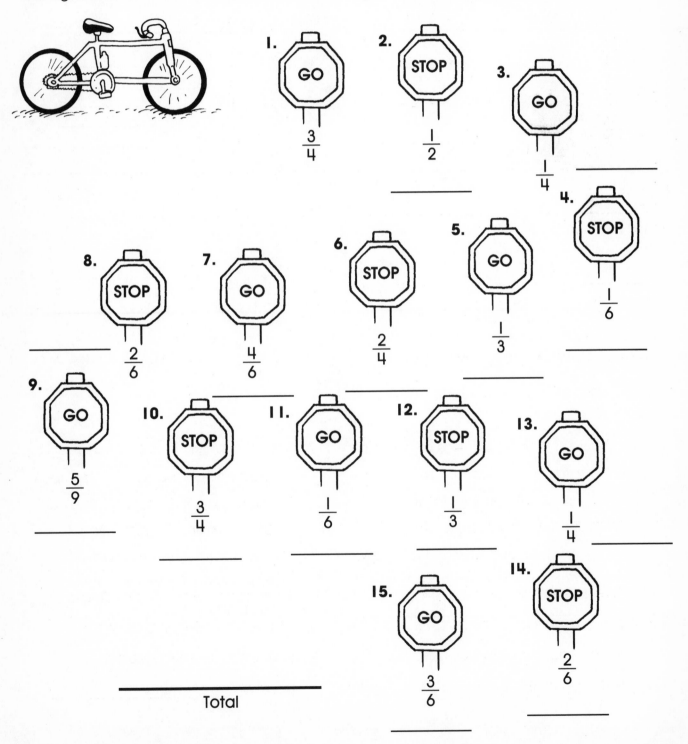

1. GO
$\frac{3}{4}$

2. STOP
$\frac{1}{2}$

3. GO
$\frac{1}{4}$

4. STOP
$\frac{1}{6}$

5. GO
$\frac{1}{3}$

6. STOP
$\frac{2}{4}$

7. GO
$\frac{4}{6}$

8. STOP
$\frac{2}{6}$

9. GO
$\frac{5}{9}$

10. STOP
$\frac{3}{4}$

11. GO
$\frac{1}{6}$

12. STOP
$\frac{1}{3}$

13. GO
$\frac{1}{4}$

14. STOP
$\frac{2}{6}$

15. GO
$\frac{3}{6}$

Total _____

Piece It Together

Add and subtract the fractions below. Reduce answers to lowest terms. Remember, some of the denominators are alike and some are different.

1. $\dfrac{3}{6} + \dfrac{29}{6} =$ _____

2. $\dfrac{41}{3} + \dfrac{29}{3} =$ _____

3. $\dfrac{5}{3} - \dfrac{1}{6} =$ _____

4. $\dfrac{7}{6} - \dfrac{2}{4} =$ _____

5. $\dfrac{11}{20} + \dfrac{46}{20} =$ _____

6. $\dfrac{7}{5} - \dfrac{2}{10} =$ _____

7. $\dfrac{3}{8} - \dfrac{1}{4} =$ _____

8. $\dfrac{5}{9} - \dfrac{3}{6} =$ _____

9. $\dfrac{14}{7} + \dfrac{3}{21} =$ _____

10. $\dfrac{1}{3} + \dfrac{3}{21} =$ _____

11. $\dfrac{10}{5} + \dfrac{3}{5} =$ _____

12. $\dfrac{8}{12} - \dfrac{6}{24} =$ _____

13. $\dfrac{32}{12} - \dfrac{8}{12} =$ _____

14. $\dfrac{1}{3} + \dfrac{6}{30} =$ _____

15. $\dfrac{10}{12} + \dfrac{52}{12} =$ _____

16. Keisha made 40 pounds of cheese. She sold $\frac{1}{2}$ that amount to a local restaurant. Because they had too much, the restaurant returned $\frac{1}{4}$ of what they purchased. With how much cheese was Keisha left?

_____

17. Dan and Sara's mom made chocolate chip cookies. Dan took $\frac{3}{6}$ of the cookies for his baseball team. Sara snuck $\frac{2}{16}$ of Dan's cookies for her friends. What fraction of the original cookies does Dan have left? _____

Climbing Pyramids

Divide fractions, starting at the bottom and working your way to the top, using the key below. Reduce each answer to lowest terms.

Key: a ÷ b = c

Multiply fractions, from the bottom to the top, using the key shown. Reduce each answer to lowest terms.

Key: a x b = c

Mix It Up

Add and subtract the mixed numbers. Reduce your answers to lowest terms.

1.
$$2\tfrac{1}{4}$$
$$+\,4\tfrac{5}{6}$$

2.
$$4\tfrac{5}{9}$$
$$+\,3\tfrac{1}{6}$$

3.
$$2\tfrac{7}{10}$$
$$+\,1\tfrac{1}{2}$$

4.
$$6\tfrac{1}{8}$$
$$+\,4\tfrac{1}{6}$$

5.
$$3\tfrac{1}{5}$$
$$-\,2\tfrac{3}{10}$$

6.
$$4\tfrac{2}{5}$$
$$-\,2\tfrac{8}{10}$$

7.
$$2\tfrac{1}{3}$$
$$+\,2\tfrac{4}{9}$$

8.
$$9\tfrac{1}{10}$$
$$-\,3\tfrac{5}{6}$$

9.
$$2\tfrac{1}{4}$$
$$+\,2\tfrac{4}{5}$$

10.
$$2\tfrac{4}{9}$$
$$-\,1\tfrac{1}{6}$$

11.
$$3\tfrac{1}{4}$$
$$+\,6\tfrac{7}{8}$$

12.
$$7\tfrac{2}{6}$$
$$-\,4\tfrac{1}{3}$$

13.
$$1\tfrac{7}{8}$$
$$+\,1\tfrac{5}{9}$$

14.
$$8\tfrac{1}{3}$$
$$+\,5\tfrac{3}{9}$$

15.
$$8\tfrac{1}{2}$$
$$+\,2\tfrac{5}{6}$$

16.
$$9\tfrac{3}{5}$$
$$+\,1\tfrac{2}{3}$$

All Mixed Up

Multiply and divide the whole numbers and fractions. Reduce to lowest terms.

1. $3 \times \dfrac{3}{4} =$ _____

2. $6 \times \dfrac{5}{6} =$ _____

3. $12 \div \dfrac{8}{5} =$ _____

4. $\dfrac{4}{5} \times 9 =$ _____

5. $\dfrac{5}{8} \times 11 =$ _____

6. $3\dfrac{1}{3} \div 2 =$ _____

7. $1\dfrac{4}{9} \times 5 =$ _____

8. $\dfrac{3}{7} \times 4\dfrac{1}{4} =$ _____

9. $2\dfrac{2}{7} \times 5 =$ _____

10. $1\dfrac{5}{7} \times 4\dfrac{1}{2} =$ _____

11. $3\dfrac{1}{6} \div 4\dfrac{2}{3} =$ _____

12. $3\dfrac{9}{10} \div 1\dfrac{1}{2} =$ _____

Name _____

Estimate Me

Estimate the following products by rounding to the nearest one and multiplying in your head. Draw a line from a multiplication problem to an estimated product. Then find the actual answer and write it on the line.

Example: 87.59 x 4.93 = 88 x 5 = 440 ← estimated product

1. 36.35 x 2.41 = _____

528

2. 40.33 x 8.01 = _____

320

3. 91.10 x 2.04 = _____

72

4. 20.60 x 10.41 = _____

114

5. 88.06 x 6.01 = _____

210

6. 29.62 x 4.05 = _____

48

7. 37.91 x 3.19 = _____

182

8. 48.30 x 1.11 = _____

120

9. 82.73 x 3.8 = _____

164

10. 41.40 x 4.11 = _____

332

Name _____

Traveling

Dena and her family took a train trip. Along the way they had to stop to let on new passengers. To find out how long the train was moving, add the decimals in the tracks, and subtract the decimals in the stop signs. Write each answer on the line. Then write the total time.

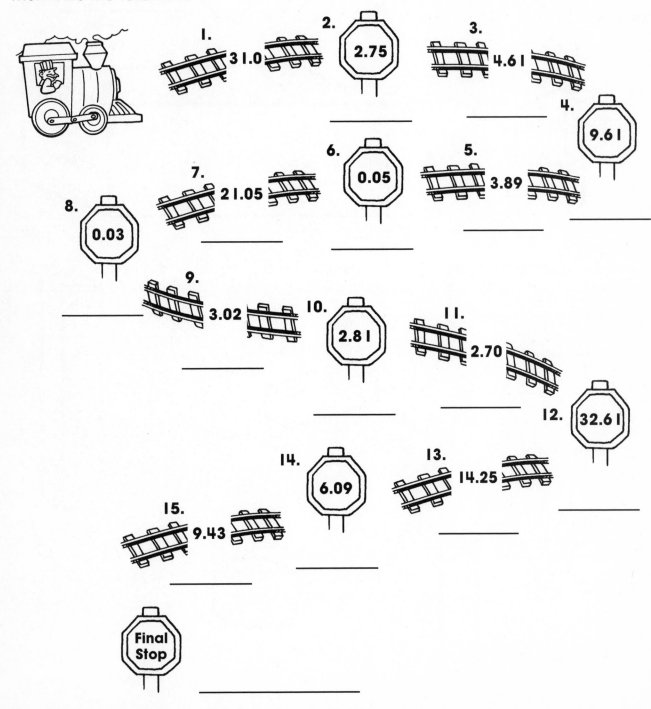

1. 31.0

2. 2.75

3. 4.61

4. 9.61

5. 3.89

6. 0.05

7. 21.05

8. 0.03

9. 3.02

10. 2.81

11. 2.70

12. 32.61

13. 14.25

14. 6.09

15. 9.43

Final Stop

Gift-Wrapped Decimals

Elena is wrapping presents, and she needs to know how many square inches of paper to buy. Find the surface area of each present. Find the area of each face (even the ones you can't see). Then add the areas. Round to the nearest hundredth of an inch. Then add the totals to find out how much paper she needs.

Grand Total : _____

1.
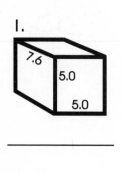
7.6
5.0
5.0
_____

2.
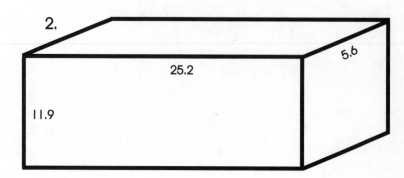
25.2
5.6
11.9
_____

3.
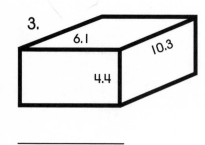
6.1
10.3
4.4
_____

5.

2.1 2.1
17.3
_____

4.
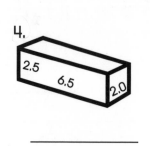
2.5
6.5
2.0
_____

6.
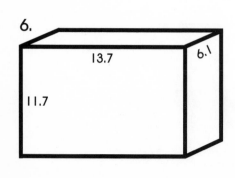
13.7
6.1
11.7
_____

7.
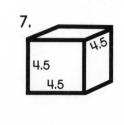
4.5
4.5
4.5
_____

Write It Out

Use paper and pencil to solve the problems below.

1. 4.4 x 1.4 = _____

2. 3.7 x 7.9 = _____

3. 0.555 x 1.5 = _____

4. 6.42 x 0.5 = _____

5. A chicken sandwich at a fast food
    restaurant has 6.3 grams of fat. If you
    eat $2\frac{1}{2}$ chicken sandwiches, how
    much fat will you eat?

    _____

6. One tablespoon of chocolate syrup
    has 27.43 calories. How many calories
    are there in 4 tablespoons?

    _____

7. One chocolate shake at a fast food
    restaurant contains 15.3 grams of fat.
    If you drink 3 shakes, how much fat
    will you consume?

    _____

Animal Trivia

To solve the riddles, solve the division problems. Then, place the corresponding letter of each answer above the problem's number below.

1. $86.25 \div 5 =$ _____

2. $42.24 \div 12 =$ _____

3. $35.5 \div 5 =$ _____

4. $1,335.2 \div 20 =$ _____

5. $266.65 \div 5 =$ _____

6. $399.99 \div 3 =$ _____

53.33	=	U
7.1	=	G
3.52	=	O
133.33	=	N
66.76	=	T
17.25	=	E

What part of a python can sense loud noises?

$$\overline{\hspace{1cm}} \quad \overline{\hspace{1cm}} \quad \overline{\hspace{1cm}} \quad \overline{\hspace{1cm}} \quad \overline{\hspace{1cm}} \quad \overline{\hspace{1cm}}$$
$$\;4 \qquad 2 \qquad 6 \qquad 3 \qquad 5 \qquad 1$$

1. $14.18 \div 4 =$ _____

2. $113.88 \div 2 =$ _____

3. $36.6 \div 6 =$ _____

4. $76.828 \div 4 =$ _____

5. $35.1 \div 5 =$ _____

6. $0.756 \div 3 =$ _____

7. $0.4998 \div 14 =$ _____

8. $583.8 \div 7 =$ _____

56.94	=	S
0.252	=	M
0.0357	=	L
83.4	=	E
7.02	=	T
19.207	=	E
6.1	=	I
3.545	=	N

From how far away can a polar bear smell a person?

$$\overline{\hspace{1cm}} \quad \overline{\hspace{1cm}} \quad \overline{\hspace{1cm}} \qquad \overline{\hspace{1cm}} \quad \overline{\hspace{1cm}} \quad \overline{\hspace{1cm}} \quad \overline{\hspace{1cm}} \quad \overline{\hspace{1cm}}$$
$$\;5 \qquad 8 \qquad 1 \qquad\quad 6 \qquad 3 \qquad 7 \qquad 4 \qquad 2$$

Nothing Corny

Solve the division problems.

1. 4 | 0.624

2. 8 | 0.08

3. 5 | 359.5

4. 2 | 76.824

5. 6 | 199.8

6. 7 | 1,803.2

7. 22 | 1,190.2

8. 3 | 298.2

9. 11 | 401.5

10. 14 | 408.8

11. 3 | 666.6

12. 9 | 193.5

13. 15 | 3.6

14. 8 | 5.232

15. 10 | 40.05

16. Noel wants to buy a bushel of corn at the farmer's market for the cheapest possible price. Look at the selections below. Determine which is the cheapest buy per bushel.

Bushel = 4 pecks

Flour corn $9.00/2 bushels
Sweet corn $5.00/peck
Waxy corn $6.00/bushel

Point the Way

Divide each numerator by its denominator to find the equal decimal value.

1. $\frac{1}{4}$ = _____

2. $\frac{27}{90}$ = _____

3. $\frac{2}{20}$ = _____

4. $\frac{1}{2}$ = _____

5. $\frac{9}{18}$ = _____

6. $\frac{5}{80}$ = _____

7. $\frac{6}{8}$ = _____

8. $\frac{4}{20}$ = _____

9. $\frac{3}{50}$ = _____

10. $\frac{26}{260}$ = _____

11. $\frac{6}{30}$ = _____

12. $\frac{12}{960}$ = _____

Delicious Decimals

The chef at the Decimal Diner can only follow recipes that use decimals as measurements. Help the chef by converting each fraction to a decimal. Round answers to the nearest tenth.

Mix Together:

$\frac{1}{4}$ cup parsley ⟶

$\frac{1}{4}$ cup basil ⟶

$\frac{1}{2}$ tablespoon vinegar ⟶

$\frac{8}{4}$ cups tomato sauce ⟶

$\frac{1}{8}$ teaspoon garlic ⟶

$\frac{3}{4}$ teaspoon salt ⟶

$\frac{1}{4}$ tablespoon chili powder ⟶

$\frac{1}{3}$ cup chopped mushrooms ⟶

$\frac{2}{4}$ cup chopped green pepper ⟶

Pour in $\frac{4}{4}$ cup cooked meatballs. ⟶

Simmer on low for 20 minutes.

Mix Together:

_____ cup parsley

_____ cup basil

_____ tablespoon vinegar

_____ cups tomato sauce

_____ teaspoon garlic

_____ teaspoon salt

_____ tablespoon chili powder

_____ cup chopped mushrooms

_____ cup chopped green pepper

Pour in _____ cup cooked meatballs.

Simmer on low for 20 minutes.

Abstract Art

The grid below contains 100 squares. Each square represents 0.01 or $\frac{1}{100}$ or 1% of all the squares. Use the table below to complete and color in the grid to achieve your own unique design.

Fill in the table below with all missing amounts.

Color	Fraction	Decimal	Percent	No. of Squares
Blue	$\frac{14}{100}$	0.14	14%	14
Purple				8
Red		0.12		
Yellow	$\frac{26}{100}$			
Green				18
Orange			22%	

Name _____

Wacky Expressions

Turn these circles into expressive faces by drawing the correct features on the circles. Match the fraction under each circle with the correct decimal, reduced fraction, and percent below.

1.

$\dfrac{12}{20}$

2.

$\dfrac{75}{100}$

3.

$\dfrac{16}{100}$

4.

$\dfrac{46}{200}$

5.

$\dfrac{85}{100}$

6.

$\dfrac{4}{100}$

Eyes	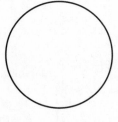 $\dfrac{3}{4}$	0.6	0.04	16%	0.23	85%
Mouths	$\dfrac{3}{5}$	$\dfrac{23}{100}$	0.16	4%	75%	0.85
Noses	$\dfrac{17}{20}$	$\dfrac{4}{25}$	60%	23%	0.75	$\dfrac{1}{25}$

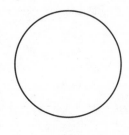
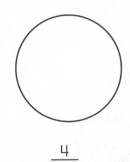
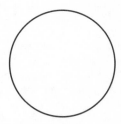
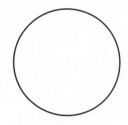
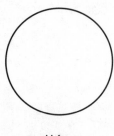

Presto Chango!

Change the following percents to decimals, and the decimals to percents.
Remember that percent means per hundred. The % sign represents hundredths,
which is the second decimal place.

1. 45% = _____

2. 75% = _____

3. 1.11 = _____

4. 0.53 = _____

5. 3.1 = _____

6. 25% = _____

7. 2.62 = _____

8. 14% = _____

9. 44% = _____

10. 1% = _____

11. 5.32 = _____

12. 555% = _____

Compare using >, <, or =.

13. 15% _____ 0.5

14. 0.04 _____ 2.5%

15. 0.01 _____ 10%

16. 3% _____ 33%

17. 1.3 _____ 13%

18. 0.5 _____ 55%

19. Rudi does magic tricks at the fair.
     In one night he entertained
     $\frac{1}{10}$ of the people in attendance.
     What percent of the people did he
     entertain? _____

20. Kerri loves to go on the Tilt-a-Whirl
     at the fair, but 80% of the time she
     has to wait in line. What decimal
     is this? _____

Name _____

Fishing Out Percents

Jeff has built an aquarium in his basement. To fill it he'll need lots of fish. Look at the fish selection and the percentage of those fish that Jeff wants. Find how many fish Jeff needs.

Fish Selection

80	Catfish
60	Clown fish
120	Guppies
80	Goldfish
150	Bluegill
24	Snails
60	Butterflyfish
300	Kissing fish
40	Angel fish
50	Mollies
70	Tetra
150	Neon fish
60	Tiger fish

Jeff Decides He Wants:

_____ 1. 30% of the Mollies

_____ 2. 46% of the Neon fish

_____ 3. 108% of the Bluegill

_____ 4. 20% of the Goldfish

_____ 5. 90% of the Butterflyfish

_____ 6. 10% of the Clown fish

_____ 7. 5% of the Catfish

_____ 8. 80% of the Guppies

_____ 9. 150% of the Snails

_____ 10. 15% of the Kissing fish

_____ 11. 75% of the Angel fish

_____ 12. 20% of the Tetra

_____ 13. 20% of the Tiger fish

_____ 14. Total Fish

15. Jeff ended up spending $3,012.48 on fish. Because he spent so much, Jeff will need to pay the bill in installments. If he pays 25% of the bill up front, how much will he have to pay each month if he pays the bill off in 6 months?

_____

Running Around in Circles

Estimate the percent of each section of each circle. Remember, the sum of the percent for each circle should equal 100%.

1. A = _____
   B = _____
   C = _____
   D = _____
   E = ___33%___

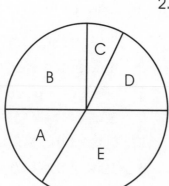

2. A = _____
   B = _____
   C = _____
   D = ___25%___
   E = _____

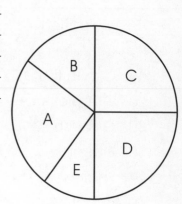

3. A = ___33%___
   B = _____
   C = _____
   D = _____

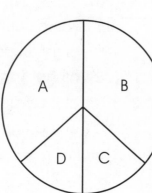

4. A = ___17%___
   B = _____
   C = _____
   D = _____
   E = ___16%___
   F = _____
   G = _____

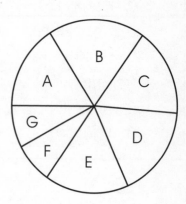

Figure the percent for each quantity and label the circles.

5. **100 Creepy Creatures**

a. 50 spiders _____

b. 12 beetles _____

c. 13 earwigs _____

d. 25 ants _____

6. **300 Favorite Sweet Treats**

a. 37 candy bars _____

b. 75 licorice _____

c. 38 gumdrops _____

d. 150 bubble gums _____

Name _____

Drive Away with Percents!

Solve each problem.

1. What is 20% of 120? _____

2. What is 10% of 72? _____

3. Cort earns 9% commission on his sales. To earn $360.00, how much must he sell?

   _____

4. Meena earns 8% commission on her sales. To earn $240.00, how much must she sell? _____

5. Michigan has 6% sales tax. How much tax is owed on a $600.00 chair? _____

6. What percent of 150 is 50? _____

7. What percent of 270 is 90? _____

8. Twenty is 50% of what number? _____

Name _____

Way Out Ratios

Start with number one and move clockwise. Fill in the blanks with the different forms of each ratio. There are three ways to write ratios: **4 to 3**, $\frac{4}{3}$, or **4 : 3**.

Name _____

Be a Sport!

A comparison of two quantities is called a ratio. Ratios can be written in three ways.

Example: Find the ratio of footballs to beach balls.   I to I   I : I $\frac{1}{1}$

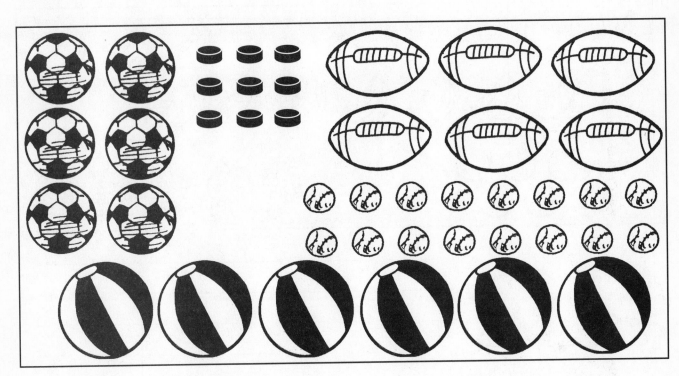

Use the box above to find the following ratios. Write each one in three ways.

1. footballs to hockey pucks   _____

2. soccer balls to beach balls   _____

3. footballs to baseballs   _____

4. hockey pucks to soccer balls   _____

5. baseballs to soccer balls   _____

Which pieces of sports equipment demonstrate the following ratios?

6. I to I   I : I $\frac{1}{1}$ _____

7. 6 to 16   6 : 16 $\frac{6}{16}$ _____

8. 9 to 16   9 : 16 $\frac{9}{16}$ _____

Name _____

Food Fun

What most looks like half of a watermelon? To find out, find the fruit ratios below. Write each ratio in three ways. Place the corresponding letter above the ratio at the bottom of the page.

E.	apples to bananas	_____
T.	oranges to grapes	_____
A.	peaches to apples	_____
O.	grapes to bananas	_____
H.	oranges to peaches	_____
E.	bananas to peaches	_____
L.	oranges to apples	_____
F.	apples to grapes	_____
H.	apples to peaches	_____
T.	grapes to peaches	_____
R.	bananas to apples	_____
H.	grapes to oranges	_____

‾‾‾‾ ‾‾‾‾ ‾‾‾‾   ‾‾‾‾ ‾‾‾‾ ‾‾‾‾ ‾‾‾‾ ‾‾‾‾
5:6   7:6   4:11   5:11   7:5   4:6   11:6   11:4

‾‾‾‾ ‾‾‾‾ ‾‾‾‾ ‾‾‾‾
5:7   6:4   7:4   4:5

Name _____

Cookie Caper

Taste-So-Good Bakery has just published a cookbook that includes sugar cookies. The following is the recipe. It makes five dozen cookies. Complete the ratio conversions below.

$2\frac{1}{4}$ cup flour $\frac{1}{3}$ cup butter

1 cup white sugar   1 tsp. baking soda

$\frac{2}{3}$ cup brown sugar   1 tsp. salt

1 tsp. vanilla   2 eggs

1. Your teacher wants to make this recipe for her parent-student night. She needs to double the recipe.

_____ cup(s) flour
_____ cup(s) white sugar
_____ cup(s) brown sugar
_____ tsp. vanilla
_____ cup(s) butter
_____ tsp. baking soda
_____ tsp. salt
_____ eggs

2. Your grandmother wants to serve sugar cookies to her reading club. She needs $1\frac{1}{3}$ of the recipe.

_____ cup(s) flour
_____ cup(s) white sugar
_____ cup(s) brown sugar
_____ tsp. vanilla
_____ cup(s) butter
_____ tsp. baking soda
_____ tsp. salt
_____ eggs

3. A Girl Scout leader needs $1\frac{1}{4}$ as much of the recipe for her troop.

_____ cup(s) flour
_____ cup(s) white sugar
_____ cup(s) brown sugar
_____ tsp. vanilla
_____ cup(s) butter
_____ tsp. baking soda
_____ tsp. salt
_____ eggs

4. Your mother wants to make sugar cookies for your aunt's baby shower. She needs $2\frac{1}{2}$ times as much.

_____ cup(s) flour
_____ cup(s) white sugar
_____ cup(s) brown sugar
_____ tsp. vanilla
_____ cup(s) butter
_____ tsp. baking soda
_____ tsp. salt
_____ eggs

Clean Out That Closet!

Help Jenny group all of her belongings into proportionate ratios. Find the pattern, then complete the table. The first one has been done for you.

Jenny's Closet							
N New Socks	O Old Socks	$\frac{N}{O}$	N : O	W White Clothes	C Color	$\frac{W}{C}$	W : C
1	3	$\frac{1}{3}$	1 : 3	2	5	$\frac{2}{5}$	2 : 5
2	6			4	10		
		$\frac{3}{9}$		8			
	12				40		
			5 : 15				32 : 80
N Nice Shoes	S Sloppy Shoes	$\frac{N}{S}$	N : S	S Stuffed Animals	B Books	$\frac{S}{B}$	S : B
			1 : 6			$\frac{3}{4}$	
2				6			
	18				16		
		$\frac{4}{24}$					24 : 32

Name _____

Ridiculous Recipes

Rita Whatintheworld is a very unusual cook. She uses strange combinations of ingredients to make very strange meals. However, the amounts of ingredients she uses are always in proportion to each other. Find the patterns on Rita's recipe card using the answers already shown and complete the table.

Rita's Brew

T tomato juice	G ginger ale	$\frac{T}{G}$	S soup	C cough syrup	$\frac{S}{C}$
4	2	$\frac{4}{2}$	3	1	
	4				$\frac{6}{2}$
12			9		
		$\frac{16}{8}$		4	
	10				$\frac{15}{5}$
24			18		
28					$\frac{21}{7}$

Setting Up Shop

Solve the following money problems.

1. Mei starts work every day at Gift Store Galore with the same amount of money in her cash register. She has: 14 ones, 5 fives, 5 twenties, 20 quarters, 50 dimes, and 50 pennies. How much is in her register?

_____

2. A customer buys 2 greeting cards for $1. 75 each and a calendar for $11.99. Mei is given a 20-dollar bill. How much change should she give back?

_____

3. Another customer purchases a hummingbird sun catcher for $15.83 and a jigsaw puzzle for $12.95. She gives Mei $30.00. How much change should the customer receive?

_____

4. Mei wants to buy a bracelet for her daughter for $29.36. She has a 20% discount as a store employee. How much does she need to pay?

_____

5. A customer is not happy with a decorative mirror she bought for $13.85 and wants to exchange it for a picture frame for $7.98. How much money should she get back?

_____

Name _____

Candy Store Story Problems

Complete the money problems below.

1. If you sold 1,600 gumballs at 10 for $0.34, how much money would you make if you sold all of them?

   _____

2. You can buy 25 candy canes for $2.50. How much money would you need to buy 300?

   _____

3. The shop owner has 1,452 gourmet chocolates that he sells 3 for $2.99. How much will he make if he sells all of them?

   _____

4. One box of chocolate truffles costs $1.25. If you buy 44 boxes, how much money would you need?

   _____

5. There are 324 peppermint swizzel sticks. You can buy 6 for $1.35. How much money would you need to buy all of them?

   _____

6. There are 120 candy bars. You can buy 6 for $3.25. How much money would you need to buy all of them?

   _____

7. The store owner has 471 bags of jawbreakers which he sells for $0.99 a bag. How much will he make if he sells all of them?

   _____

8. The shopkeeper has 253 bags of licorice. He sells 11 bags for $1.99. How much money will he earn if he sells all of the bags?

   _____

9. There are 40 pieces of candy corn in a bag. Each bag costs $0.50. If there are 640 total pieces of candy corn, how many bags are there? How much would it cost to buy all of the candy corn?

   _____

Two-Stepping

Solve each word problem.

1. If you buy 2 cheese sandwich lunches at $0.95 each, plus a $0.75 soda, and give the cashier $5.00, how much change should you get back?

    _____

2. Your teacher treated each of the 27 students in your class to a fast food lunch for $1.95 each, plus 2 lunches for herself. She had $60.00. How much change does she get?

    _____

3. You bought white milk at $0.25 for 20 days. Your friend bought chocolate milk at $0.35 for 20 days. How much more did your friend spend in all?

    _____

4. You collected 887 baseball cards. Your friend collected 10 times as many, as well as 34 comic books. How many items did your friend collect?

    _____

5. The school cook uses 1,440 chocolate chips to make 480 cookies. Each chip costs $0.02. How much does it cost to add chocolate chips to each cookie?

    _____

6. Each burger is topped with 4 pickles. Each cheeseburger is topped with 2 slices of cheese. If 1 order is placed for 437 burgers, and another order is placed for 758 cheeseburgers, which order will have the most toppings? How much more?

    _____

7. In 1 week the candy store sold 737 gumballs at $0.03 each. They also sold 469 candy corns at $0.05 each. Which candy brought in the most money and how much more? _____

No Problem Story Problems

Use the correct operations to solve each problem.

1. Tonya sold 415 doughnuts last week and made $124.50. This week she sold 217 doughnuts. How many doughnuts did she sell in all? How much does each doughnut cost?

    _____

2. Jeremy built a house of cards using 119 red cards and 43 black cards. Twenty-three red cards fell over. Thirty-seven black cards also fell over. How many cards in all were left standing? _____

3. Lisa and Jun were excited about selling cookies. Lisa sold 306 boxes and made $918. Jun made $1,530. How many boxes did Jun sell? _____

4. Grandma Ann made apple and cherry pies to sell at the county fair. She sold 87 apple pies for $4.25 each and 163 cherry pies for $5.00 each. How many pies did she sell all together? How much did she earn? _____

5. Jamal made 109 red bookmarks and 58 yellow bookmarks for the school library. Ninety-three students wanted red and 75 wanted yellow. How many red bookmarks were left? How many students didn't get a yellow one that wanted one?

    _____

    _____

6. Last week Surya helped 217 customers at the shoe store. Of the total number of customers, 103 were men and 45 were children. How many customers were women? _____

7. Dahlila helped her father sell 175 quarts of raspberries and 59 quarts of strawberries for $2.29 a quart. How many quarts were sold in all? How much did they earn?

    _____

8. Maria and her sister, Lidia, made flowers out of different colors of tissue paper for the school float. Maria made 314 red flowers, and Lidia made 107 yellow flowers. Only 251 red flowers and 79 yellow flowers were used. How many red flowers were left? How many yellow flowers were left? _____

    _____

Hanging Out with Mental Math

Using mental math, solve the following problems.

1. Amber wanted to buy a pair of pants that cost $21.65 and a shirt for $17.75. About how much would both pieces cost? Amber only had $32.00. Did she have enough?

    _____

    _____

2. Arun wanted to buy a comic book for $0.39, a collection of baseball cards for $7.75, and a soda for $0.70. About how much money did he need? _____

3. Tamara and Reuben made bookmarks to sell at the school bazaar for $0.73 each, and they sold 121 of them. About how much money did they raise for their school?

    _____

4. Chin sold her skates for $17.23 and bought a CD for $14.72. About how much money did she have left?

    _____

5. Sofia counted 6 peanuts in each cookie. About how many nuts are there in 4 dozen cookies?

    _____

6. The average school supply bill for Fun Elementary is $2,984.00 per month. About how much money is spent on supplies in 12 months?

    _____

Name _____

Review of Story Problems

Use the correct operations to solve each problem.

1. After school, Tony helped work at his dad's collector shop. They sold 517 baseball cards the first week for $0.12 each. The second week they sold 329. How many cards did they sell in all? _____

2. Dana constructed a trail of 968 dominoes for her science project. Of this number, 348 were black. The rest were red. Suddenly, 217 black dominoes and half of the red dominoes fell over. How many dominoes fell over? _____

3. In a class of 27 students, everyone was required to work on writing a puppet show. Four of the students were then given permission to work on set design instead of writing. Two students were absent on that day. The teacher asked only the students writing to break up into groups of 3. How many writing groups were formed? _____

4. The average number of hours people sleep is 7. How many hours of sleeping are there in a 30-night period? If everyone decided to sleep $1\frac{1}{2}$ extra hours each night, how many more hours of sleeping would occur in a 30-night period?

   _____

5. A chef uses 2,400 walnuts to make 400 walnut brownies. Each walnut costs $0.02. How much does it cost to add walnuts to each brownie?

   _____

6. Three hundred ninety-nine orders of submarine sandwiches use 4 pickles per order. Eight hundred ten orders of ham and cheese sub sandwiches use 2 slices of cheese per order. Which sandwich order uses the most toppings?

   _____

7. In 1 class, 12 students wore hats on "Hats and Shades Day" while 7 times as many students wore shades. How many more students wore shades? _____

8. Nina helped her grandma sell 165 quarts of blueberries for $1.79 per quart and 79 quarts of raspberries for $2.25 per quart. How many quarts were sold in all? How much more did they make selling blueberries than raspberries?

   _____

Make Cents?

Read each situation and decide if it makes sense. If so, write **yes**. If not, state the error that is made and correct the problem.

1. Irina has the opportunity to buy a $75.00 computer game on sale for 20% off. If she pays cash, she receives an additional 5% off the sale price. Irina figures she will pay $57.00 in cash for the computer game.

    _____
    _____

2. A $180.00 bicycle on sale for 15% off is marked $155.00.

    _____
    _____

3. The troop membership went from 50 to 80 members and then dropped down to 50. Liang stated that the percent of decrease was the same as the percent of increase.

    _____
    _____

4. A pair of $75.00 in-line skates on sale for 30% off is marked $52.50.

    _____
    _____

5. Brent can buy 2 $15.00 CDs on sale for 15% off, or he can take advantage of the Buy One, Get One-Half-Off special. He figures he will save more with the half-off special.

    _____
    _____

Name _____

Factoring Out

Find the prime factors of the members at the top of these graphic trees. The first one has been done for you.

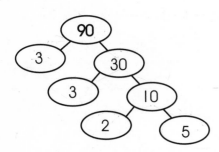

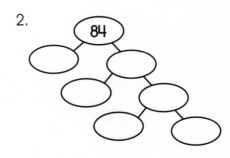

1.

2.

Prime Factors: __3, 3, 2, 5__
$3 \times 3 \times 2 \times 5 = 90$

Prime Factors: _____

_____

Prime Factors: _____

_____

3.

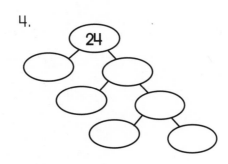

4.

5.

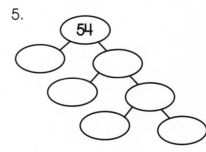

Prime Factors: _____

_____

Prime Factors: _____

_____

Prime Factors: _____

_____

6.

7.

8.

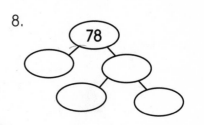

Prime Factors: _____

_____

Prime Factors: _____

_____

Prime Factors: _____

_____

IF87127 *Standards-Based Math*

Bubble Trouble

To find the greatest common factor, find the prime factors and multiply.

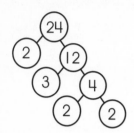

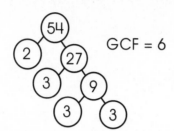

GCF = 6

| Prime Factors for 24: ⟨2, 3,⟩ 2, 2 |
| Prime Factors for 54: ⟨2, 3,⟩ 3, 3 |
| 2 x 3 = 6   GCF = 6 |

1.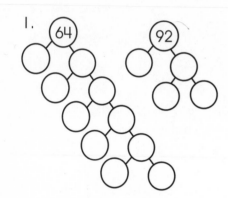

Prime Factors for 64:

_____

Prime Factors for 92:

_____

GCF = _____

2.

Prime Factors for 24:

_____

Prime Factors for 18:

_____

GCF = _____

3.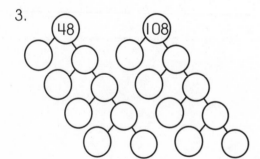

Prime Factors for 48:

_____

Prime Factors for 108:

_____

GCF = _____

4.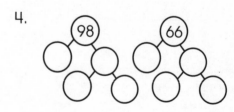

Prime Factors for 98:

_____

Prime Factors for 66:

_____

GCF = _____

Name _____

Exciting Exponents

When you see a figure like 5^2, the 2 is the exponent and the 5 is the base. This means that the 5 is multiplied by itself two times. Fill in the crossword with solutions written in word form.

Across

1. $6^2 + 4 = $ _____
2. $4^2 - 2 = $ _____
3. $2^2 + 7 = $ _____

Down

1. $8^2 - 14 = $ _____
2. $4^2 \div 4 = $ _____
3. $7^2 + 11 = $ _____
4. $3^2 - 6 = $ _____
5. $20^2 - 399 = $ _____

Multiply Out

Circle numbers on the spokes that are multiples of the number in the circle.

1.
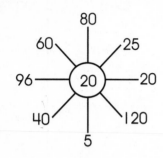

2.
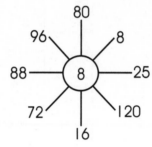

3.
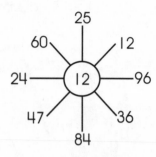

4.
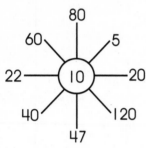

5.

```
        80
   96        8
  88    8    25
   72       120
        16
```

6.

```
        16
  121       96
  64    16   32
   85       71
        48
```

7.

```
        14
   42        2
  84    14   56
   70       44
        28
```

8.

```
        88
    5        11
   99   11   17
   22        1
        55
```

9.

```
        90
    5        3
   60   30   30
   15       120
        6
```

Replace each letter with the correct number.

10. $5^2 + 3 = y$

   y = _____

11. $12^2 \div 2 = b$

   b = _____

12. $7 + 4^2 = c$

   c = _____

13. $3^2 + 6 = h$

   h = _____

14. $5^2 \div 5 = i$

   i = _____

15. $3^2 - 0 = x$

   x = _____

16. $4^2 = p$

   p = _____

17. $30^2 - 800 = m$

   m = _____

Name _____

What's the Pattern?

1. Look at these three instances of a pattern. Describe the pattern in words.

$$\frac{5}{5} = 1 \qquad \frac{45.5}{45.5} = 1 \qquad \frac{n}{n} = 1$$

_____

_____

2. Look at these three instances of a pattern.

$$\frac{1}{2} \quad + \quad \frac{1}{4} \quad = \quad \frac{1}{4} \quad + \quad \frac{1}{2}$$

$$36 \quad + \quad 24 \quad = \quad 24 \quad + \quad 36$$

$$4.5 \quad + \quad 2.42 \quad = \quad 2.42 \quad + \quad 4.5$$

a. Describe this pattern in words. _____

_____

b. Show this pattern with variables. _____

_____

3. Look at these three instances of a pattern.

4 kilometers = 4,000 meters

0.2 kilometers = 200 meters

$\frac{1}{2}$ kilometer = 500 meters

a. Describe this pattern in words. _____

_____

b. Write a numerical expression with variables to represent this pattern. _____

_____

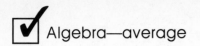

Name _____

Penny Counter

Each day, Dena counts a different number of pennies. Add the numbers in the matrix to find out how many. Then add the totals on the right and divide by 7 to find out the average number of pennies Dena counted each day for a week.

862	+	12	=
+		+	
5	+	461	=
=		=	
	+		=
+		+	
51	+	63	=
=		=	
	+		=
+		+	
114	+	35	=
=		=	
	+		=

Total _____

Average _____

What Do You Mean by Median?

The **mean** is the average found by adding all values and dividing by the number of values. The **median** is the number that is exactly in the middle of the data.

Example: Lenny loves basketball. He scored the following points per game.

Game	Points
#1	5
#2	10
#3	3
#4	14
#5	3

Median: 3, 3, ⑤ 10, 14
The median is 5 points per game.

Mean: 5 + 10 + 3 + 14 + 3 = 35
   35 ÷ 5 = 7
The mean is an average of 7 points per game.

Study the data to correctly answer the questions.

Student	No. of books read
Anna	9
Carlos	5
Brian	7
Jada	8
Lin	11

1. List the numbers you would add and what you would divide them by to determine the mean number of books read by each student.

   _____

2. What is the mean? _____

3. What is the median? _____

Tanya's scout troop made beaded animals to sell and raise funds for a camping trip.

Troop Members	No. of bead animals made
Tanya	17
Cho	15
María	11
Avishai	14
Lucy	9
Kely	6
Yong	21
Maya	6
Beth	9

4. List the numbers you would add and what you would divide them by to determine the mean number of beaded animals made by each troop member.

   _____

   _____

5. What is the mean? _____

6. What is the median? _____

Name _____

Numerical Expressions

Look at each numerical expression below. First, solve powers. Next, solve each multiplication and division problem in order from left to right. Then solve each addition and subtraction problem in order from left to right. Write each separate equation involved in solving and solve. See the example for help.

Example: $3^4 \times 2 - 6 =$

$3 \times 3 \times 3 \times 3 = 81$

$81 \times 2 = 162$

$162 - 6 = \boxed{156}$

1. $9^2 - 2 \times 24 =$ _____

2. $100 \div 5 \times 3 =$ _____

3. $4 \times 11 - 6 \times 2 =$ _____

4. $3.478 \times 2^2 =$ _____

Evaluate the following pairs of operations. Circle the one that you would complete first.

5. division and subtraction

6. a power and multiplication

7. addition and subtraction

8. multiplication and addition

Solve the following. Show your work.

9. $5^2 + 8^6 =$ _____

10. $2,500 - 10 \times 12^2 =$ _____

Name _____

Order Up!

Complete the equations below, making sure you follow the order of operations.

> 1. First, do parentheses, then brackets.
> 2. Next, do multiplication and division, in order from left to right.
> 3. Finally, do addition and subtraction, in order from left to right.

1. $35 + 50 + \dfrac{25}{5} \cdot 5 - (8 + 11) =$ _____

2. $^-16 + (20 \cdot 6) \div (6 + 2) + 31 =$ _____

3. $3 \cdot 2 [4 + (9 \div 3)] =$ _____

4. $2 + [48 \div (12 + 4)] - 16 =$ _____

5. $2[^-6(3 - 12) - 17] =$ _____

6. $\dfrac{1}{2} (^-16 - 4) =$ _____

7. $50 \div [(4 \cdot 5) - (36 \div 2)] + {}^-91 =$ _____

8. $[5(20 - 2)] \div \dfrac{30}{2} + 6 - 3 =$ _____

Writing Algebraic Expressions

Write the following word expressions as numerical expressions and vice versa.

1. 5 less than a number _____

2. 6 times a number plus 7 times the number _____

3. $\frac{2}{3}$ of a number minus 11 _____

4. 10 more than the quotient of c and 3 _____

5. the product of 9 and a number, decreased by 7 _____

6. $2(c - 4)$ _____

7. $2 + 6b$ _____

8. $3(a + 12)$ _____

9. y^5 _____

10. $4 \cdot 5 + z$ _____

11. Write a word and numerical algebraic expression with an answer that is your age.

   _____

   _____

Express It

Write each algebraic expression below as a word expression.

Example:	y + 4
	A number plus 4, or
	The sum of a number and 4, or
	A number increased by 4

1. y – 6 _____

2. $\dfrac{x}{5}$ _____

3. l • w • h _____

4. c + 0.50 _____

5. 24 – b _____

6. 2n + 3 _____

Write several word expressions for the following operation signs.

7. + _____

8. x _____

9. ÷ _____

10. – _____

11. = _____

12. ⌐‾ _____

Name _____

Simplifying Expressions

Simplify each of the following expressions using the distributive property and by combining like terms.

1. $^-7(a + b)$ _____

2. $x(y - 4)$ _____

3. $-\frac{2}{3}(c - 120)$ _____

4. $^-8(\frac{t}{2} + 6)$ _____

5. $3(a + b) + 2b$ _____

6. $8 - 3(6 - 6x)$ _____

7. $6m + 7(7m + 9)$ _____

8. $^-6 \cdot {}^-2 ({}^-5x + 9 - 3x)$ _____

Solving

Solve the following.

1. $a + {}^-7 = 8$ _____

2. $30 = b - {}^-2$ _____

3. $5.62 = m - 6$ _____

4. $y + {}^-6.2 = 8.1$ _____

5. $2.4 = m + 3.7$ _____

6. $P - \dfrac{3}{5} = \dfrac{3}{5}$ _____

7. ${}^-12 + x = 21$ _____

8. $a - 18 = {}^-32$ _____

It Varies

Solve for the variable.

1. $-6a = -66$ _____

2. $1.5 = 3x$ _____

3. $8 = 32b$ _____

4. $9a = -3$ _____

5. $28 = a \div 13$ _____

6. $u \div -4 = -14$ _____

7. $x \div 7 = 35$ _____

8. $-13n = 13$ _____

9. $\dfrac{x}{6} = 6$ _____

10. $0.12 = y \div 0.12$ _____

Solve the following word problems.

11. Martin works in a youth day camp during the summer. Each day he must bring 3 pieces of fruit per child. On this day, Martin brings 135 pieces of fruit. Can you tell how many children went to camp? Write a division and a multiplication equation, using variables, to show how you would solve this problem. Then solve.

_____
_____
_____

12. Hua is the refreshments coordinator for the student council. Each week the council meets on Thursday to discuss school issues and then have a snack. Hua always brings 2 cups of snacks per council member. However, the number of members present at the meeting varies each week. Write 1 multiplication and 1 division equation, using variables, that will help Hua quickly find the total cups of snacks once she knows the number of members present.

_____
_____

Name _____

Amazing Algebra

Find the value of the variable.

1. a x 51 = 2,601

   a = _____

2. g ÷ 93 = 4

   g = _____

3. 663 ÷ b = 3

   b = _____

4. 61 x 19 = h

   h = _____

5. 1,365 − c = 951

   c = _____

6. 2i + 14 = 28

   i = _____

7. 216 + 56 = d

   d = _____

8. 30m − 600 = 300

   m = _____

9. e x 42 = 1,008

   e = _____

10. 1,249 − 75 = k

    k = _____

Name _____

Expressive Equations

Solve for each letter.

1. a = (b − c) • a ÷ c   a = _____   b = __6__   c = _____
    a ÷ c = 3
    c + c + c = a
    c < 4
    4 < a < 10

2. d ÷ (e − f) − (g • h) = h   h = _____   g = _____   e = _____
    e = f + f   f = __4__   d = _____
    f = g x g
    1 < g < 3
    d ÷ (e − f) = 6

3. I = (I + J) − (K ÷ L)   J = _____   I = _____   K = __20__
    I + J = 14   L = _____
    4 < L < 6
    K ÷ L = J
    J = 4

4. m = (n − m) • o ÷ p   n = _____   o = __4__   p = _____
    n − m = o   m = _____
    3 < o < 5
    n = 12
    p + p = o

5. q = (r + s) − (t • u)   q = _____   r = _____   s = _____
    u + u = r   t = _____   u = __2__
    3 < r < 5
    t x u = 10
    r + s = 10

Name _____

What If?

Find the answer for each equation below given the change in the variable.

1. $a + 59 = \underline{b}$

a	b
20	
103	
98	

2. $48 \div x = \underline{y}$

x	y
4	
8	
6	

3. $4h = \underline{g}$

h	g
1.5	
8	
112	

4. $124 - c = \underline{d}$

c	d
40	
35.7	
$\frac{1}{2}$	

5. $5\underline{t} = u$

u	t
35	
452.5	
$\frac{1}{5}$	

6. $\underline{r} + 385 = s$

s	r
577.5	
45,857	
385^2	

7. Josiah is planning a back-yard garden, but isn't sure what dimensions he wants. He knows he wants the length to be 3 times the width. Find the area of his garden given the three different widths below.

a. 10 ft. _____

b. 14.5 sq. ft. _____

c. 5.75 sq. ft. _____

Name _____

Expressing Ourselves

Find the value of each expression below given each substitution.

1. Find the value of $46 - 48 \times n$ when:

    a. $n = 1$ _____

    b. $n = 2$ _____

2. Find the value of $12 \cdot 2n$ when:

    a. $n = 2$ _____

    b. $n = 4$ _____

3. Find the value of $48 \div n + 2^2$ when:

    a. $n = 2$ _____

    b. $n = 6$ _____

4. Find the value of each expression if $n = 6$

    a. $24 - n^2 =$ _____

    b. $28 - 2n + n =$ _____

    c. $n^6 =$ _____

5. Find the value of each expression if $n = 2$.

    a. $96 \div n^2 =$ _____

    b. $n + n^2 - n =$ _____

    c. $5n^4 =$ _____

Name _____

Evaluating Expressions

Evaluate the following if $a = \frac{1}{2}$, $x = 4$, and $y = -2$.

1. $4(a - 1) =$ _____

2. $4a - 3y =$ _____

3. $4(x - 3y) =$ _____

4. $x(a + 6) =$ _____

5. $x(ax + ay) =$ _____

6. $xy(2a + 3x - 2) =$ _____

Name _____

Mixed Practice

Solve for the variable.

1. $x + 12 = 8$ $x =$ _____   2. $-23 + w = 48$ $w =$ _____

3. $\dfrac{y}{-6} = 2$ $y =$ _____   4. $9 = 54m$ $m =$ _____

5. $-10 = m - 6$ $m =$ _____   6. $\dfrac{1}{16x} = 8$ $x =$ _____

7. $2.7 = 3y$ $y =$ _____   8. $-42 = y - 20$ $y =$ _____

9. $-1 = \dfrac{r}{20}$ $r =$ _____   10. $92 + x = 92$ $x =$ _____

Name _____

Shapes Face Off

Congruent shapes are the same size and shape. Similar shapes are the same shape but not always the same size. Write congruent or similar below each set of shapes.

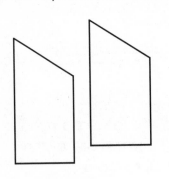

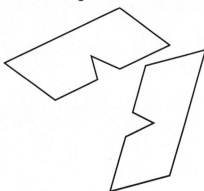

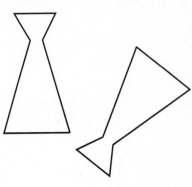

1._____   2._____   3._____

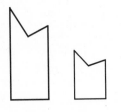

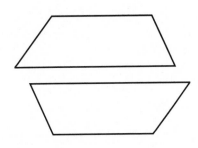

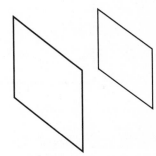

4._____   5._____   6._____

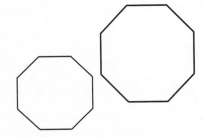

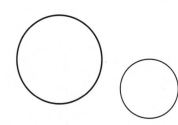

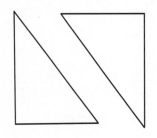...

7._____   8._____   9._____

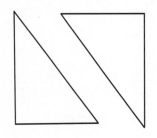

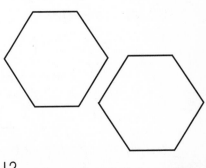

10._____   11._____   12._____

73   IF87127 *Standards-Based Math*

Name _____

Similar Sensation

The example below compares a large shape to a small one.

Example: $\overline{AC}$ corresponds to $\overline{EG}$, or $\dfrac{\overline{AC}}{\overline{EG}}$

$$\frac{\overline{AC}}{\overline{EG}} = \frac{10}{5} = \frac{2}{1} = 2$$

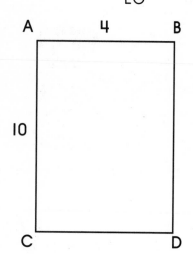

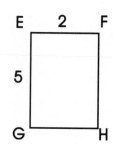

So, the large polygon is 2 times the size of the small polygon.

Use one corresponding pair of segments in the similar polygons to fill in the blanks.

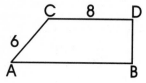   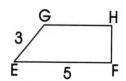

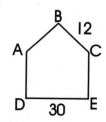

1. $\dfrac{\overline{AC}}{\overline{EG}}$ = _____

2. The small polygon is _____ the size of the larger.

3. If E to F = 5, what is the length of A to B? _____

4. If C to D = 8, what is the length of G to H? _____

5. How many right angles does each polygon have? _____

6. $\dfrac{\overline{DE}}{\overline{IJ}}$ = _____

7. The larger polygon is _____ times the size of the smaller polygon.

8. If B to C = 12, what is the length of G to H? _____

9. If H to J = 5, what is the length of C to E? _____

10. How many acute angles does each polygon have? _____

Name _____

Mirror Image

Draw a dotted line to make each shape symmetrical. Some shapes can have more than one line of symmetry. The first one has been done for you.

1.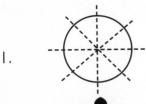

2.

3.

4.

5.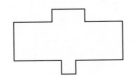

6.

7.

8.

9.

Each of these letters has been cut on a line of symmetry. Match each letter half with its twin. Draw a line from one half to the other.

Can you identify each letter? Write each letter on the blanks below.

____ ____ ____ ____ ____ ____

Write the mirror image of each letter half below. Then read the words.

BOX   COOK   KICK

Name _____

Points, Lines, and Planes

Look at the plane. Write true or false for the following statements.

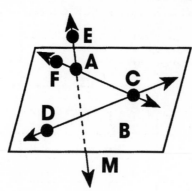

_____ 1. $\overleftrightarrow{AC} \cap \overleftrightarrow{DC} = C$

_____ 2. E lies on B.

_____ 3. Points A, C, and F are collinear.

_____ 4. Points A, C, and F are coplanar.

_____ 5. $\overleftrightarrow{DC}$ lies in B.

_____ 6. Point A lies on M and B.

_____ 7. A line can be drawn containing points D and E.

_____ 8. A line can be drawn containing points A, C, and E.

_____ 9. Any line contained in plane B intersects $\overleftrightarrow{CF}$.

_____ 10. A plane exists that contains points A, D, and E.

Tell whether each set of points is collinear or noncollinear; coplanar or noncoplanar.

11. A, B, C

12. G, H, E, B

_____

_____

13. D, E, H

14. B, H

_____

_____

15. A, D, G, H

16. A, B, F, H

_____

_____

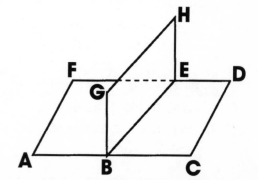

Plotting Points

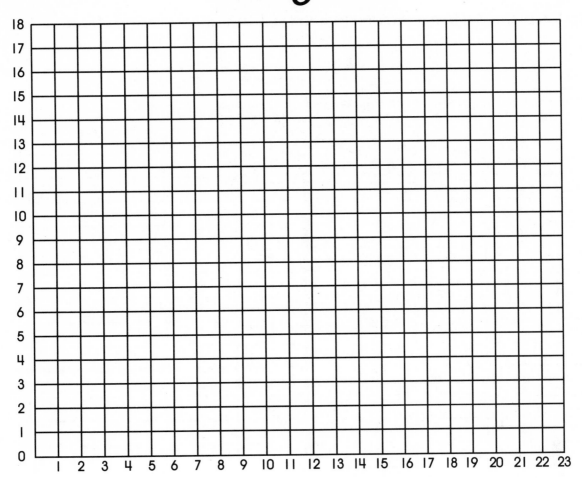

Figure 1

A = (1, 17)	E = (7, 11)
B = (1, 14)	F = (7, 14)
C = (1, 11)	G = (7, 17)
D = (4, 12)	H = (4, 16)

Figure 2

I = (5, 8)	M = (11, 2)
J = (6, 5)	N = (10, 5)
K = (5, 2)	O = (11, 8)
L = (8, 2)	P = (8, 8)

Plot the points noted to create two figures on the graph. Connect each point with lines in the order given and label Figures 1 and 2.

1. How many sides and how many vertices does each shape have? _____
2. Draw two line segments for each shape that represent lines of symmetry. Write the names of the line segments. _____
3. Are these figures congruent or similar? _____
4. What shapes could you put together to create either figure? Give two possible solutions. _____

_____

Ship Shape

Study each set and draw points on the graph according to the coordinates given. The order of each coordinate is (x, y). Then connect the dots in order to form geometric shapes. The first one is done for you.

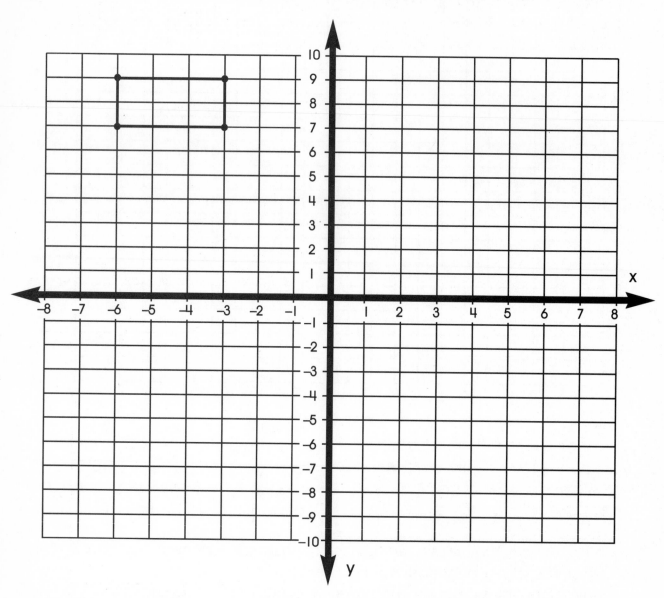

1. (−6, 7) (−6, 9) (−3, 7) (−3, 9)

2. (−5, 3) (−3, 5) (−1, 3)

3. (−7, −4) (−6, −2) (−4, −4) (−3, −2)

4. (−5, −5) (−3, −8) (−2, −5)

5. (2, 2) (2, 3) (7, 2) (7, 3)

6. (2, 5) (2, 7) (3, 4) (3, 8) (5, 4) (6, 5) (6, 7) (5, 8)

7. (3, −2) (3, −6) (5, −2) (5, −6)

8. (2, −9) (3, −7) (5, −7) (6, −9)

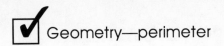

Name _____

Puzzling Perimeters

Jason was helping to build a tennis court at a local park. Help him take measurements to buy materials.

Perimeter = the distance around a shape
P = side + side + side + side

15 feet

9 feet   Tennis Court   9 feet

15 feet

1. Using the perimeter formula, find the perimeter of the court . _____

2. Fencing is sold in sections of 3 feet. How many sections will Jason need to buy to go around the entire court?

    _____

3. Each section of fencing costs $3.95. How much will the fencing cost in all?

    _____

4. The park service decides to build a spectator area near the court. Jason wants it to be a perfect square. Can you find the perimeter?

    _____

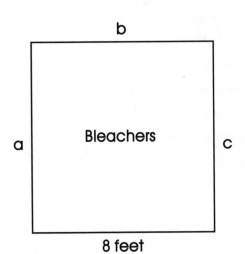

b

a   Bleachers   c

8 feet

5. What is the total length of a, b, and c? _____

6. How many sections of fencing will Jason need to buy to fit around the bleachers?

    _____

Name _____

Size It Up

Find the perimeter of each quadrilateral below and write it in the center of the shape.

1.
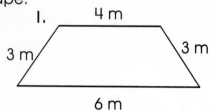
4 m
3 m   3 m
6 m

2.
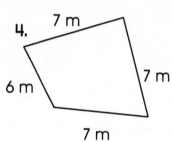
19 m
18 m   18m
19 m

3.
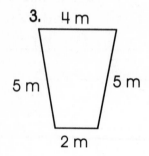
4 m
5 m   5 m
2 m

4.
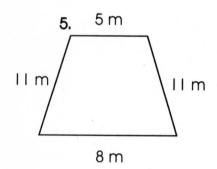
7 m
6 m   7 m
7 m

5.
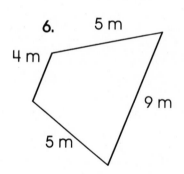
5 m
11 m   11 m
8 m

6.
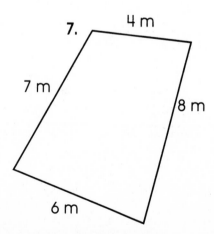
5 m
4 m
9 m
5 m

7.
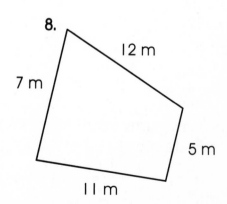
4 m
7 m
8 m
6 m

8.
12 m
7 m
5 m
11 m

Name _____

Is It Right?

Shade all the triangles that have the correct area. Correct the areas that are wrong.

$$\text{Area} = \frac{1}{2} \text{ base x height}$$

1.

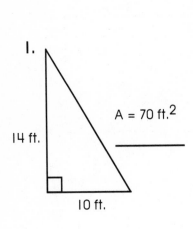

A = 70 ft.^{2}

14 ft.

10 ft.

_____

2.

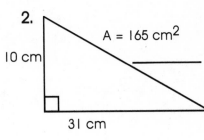

A = 165 cm^2

10 cm

31 cm

_____

3.

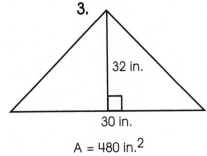

32 in.

30 in.

A = 480 in.^{2}

_____

4.

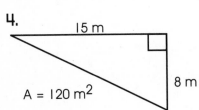

15 m

8 m

A = 120 m^2

_____

5.

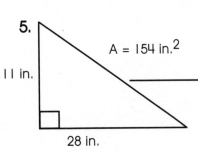

A = 154 in.^{2}

11 in.

28 in.

_____

6.

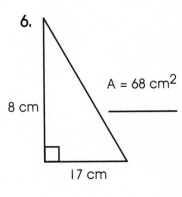

A = 68 cm^2

8 cm

17 cm

_____

7.

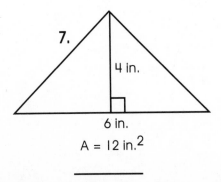

4 in.

6 in.

A = 12 in.^{2}

_____

8.

8 mm

10 mm

A = 16 mm^2

_____

81   IF87127 *Standards-Based Math*

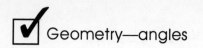
What's My Angle?

Find the missing angle measurements in each triangle using the measurements given.

A = _____   H = _____
B = _____   I = _____
C = _____   J = _____
D = _____   K = _____
E = _____   L = _____
F = _____   M = _____
G = _____

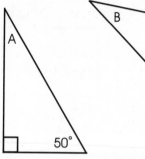
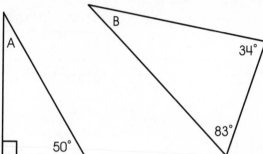
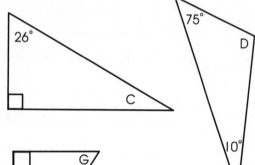
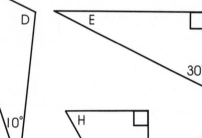
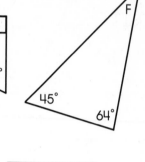
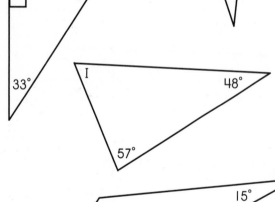
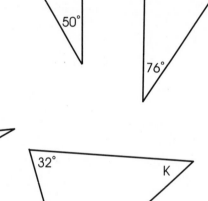
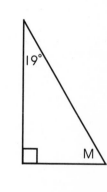

1. How many are obtuse triangles? _____

2. How many are acute triangles? _____

3. How many are right triangles? _____

Name _____

Sail Away with Angles

Look at each triangle. Use the measurements given to write the kind of triangle on the line (**right**, **acute**, or **obtuse**). Then, find the missing angle. Put the corresponding letter of the angle above its measurement at the bottom of the page to answer the riddle.

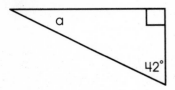

Example: a = 180° − (90° + 42°) = 48°

_____Right_____

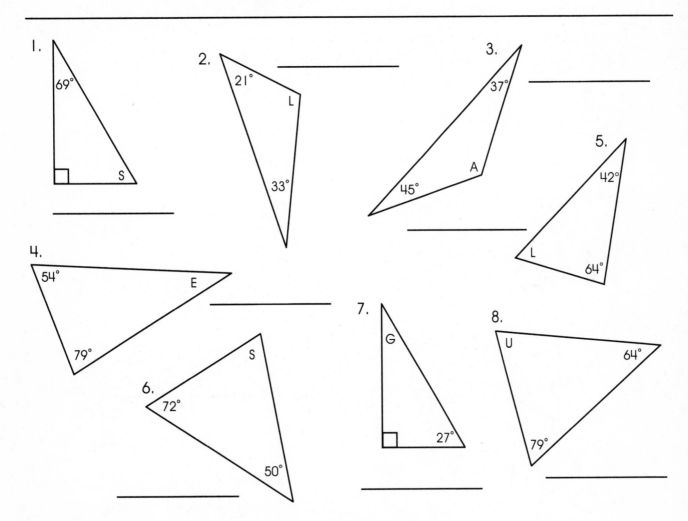

Which scavenger birds love the water and French fries?

___ ___ ___ ___ ___ ___ ___ ___
21° 47° 98° 63° 37° 74° 126° 58°

Triangles

Scalene
No equal sides

Right
1 right angle

Isosceles = 1 right angle
Equilateral = 3 equal sides

Acute
3 acute angles

Obtuse
1 obtuse angle

Equiangular
3 angles each = 60°

Classify each triangle below by writing the name on the line.

1. _____

2. _____

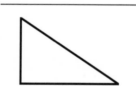

3. _____

4. _____

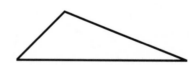

5.

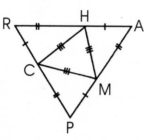

a. Name all equilateral triangles.

_____

b. Name all isosceles triangles.

_____

c. Name all scalene triangles.

_____

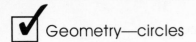

Name _____

Exploring Circumference and Diameter

Study the definitions in the term box and look closely at the circle to understand and answer the questions below.

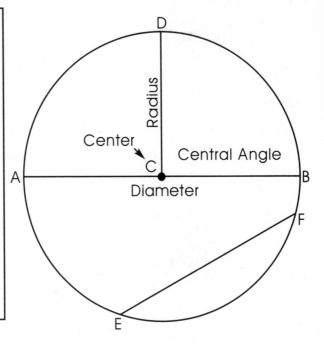

Terms

Circumference: the distance around a circle

Diameter: a segment connecting two points on a circle and going through the center of the circle.

Radius: a line segment connecting the center of a circle to any point on the circle

Central Angle: an angle whose vertex is at the center of a circle

Center: a point such that every point on the circle is the same distance from it

Chord: any line segment that connects two points on a circle

List the line segments for the following. Remember to draw a line over the two letters to represent a segment. For example: $\overline{NO}$

1. Radius: _____

2. Diameter: _____

3. Chord: _____

4. What is the measurement of the central angle? _____

5. If the radius is 3.5 feet, what is the diameter? _____

6. If the diameter is 4 feet and 12 inches, what is the radius?

_____

7. If the radius is 9 yards, how many inches is the diameter?

_____

8. If the diameter is 4 feet and 18 inches, how long is the radius?

_____

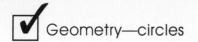

Name _____

Diameter v. Circumference

The Greek symbol for pi is π. We use 3.14 as the value for pi. In any circle, the circumference divided by the diameter equals pi. We can use pi to find the circumference or diameter. Complete the table below by filling in any missing values. Remember to round your answer to the nearest tenth of a centimeter. The first row has been done for you.

Diameter	Circumference	$\frac{C}{D}$	C ÷ D
11 cm	34.5 cm	$\frac{34.5}{11}$	3.14
	8.8 cm		3.14
6 cm			3.14
	47.1 cm		
		$\frac{25.1}{8}$	3.14
9 cm			3.14
	37.7 cm		
		$\frac{9.4}{3}$	3.14
4 cm			3.14
	21.9 cm		

Name _____

Concept Review of Circles

Complete the following.

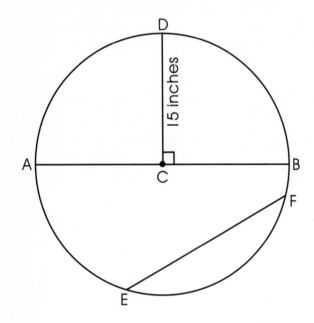

1. $\overline{AB}$ = _____

2. What is the term for the distance around a circle? _____

3. What is the measurement of the diameter? _____

4. What line segment is called a chord?

   _____

5. $\overline{CD}$ = _____

6. What is the measurement of the central angle? _____

Complete the chart. Round to the nearest tenth.

Diameter	Circumference	$\dfrac{C}{D}$	C ÷ D	Radius
			3.14	8 cm
	48.6 cm			
9 cm				
		$\dfrac{18.84}{6}$		
				4 cm
	12.6 cm		3.14	

Name _____

Area

Triangle:	area = $\frac{1}{2}$ base x height
Rectangle/Square:	area = base x height
Parallelogram:	area = base x height
Trapezoid:	area = $\frac{1}{2}$ height (base + base)

Find the area of the polygonal regions below. Express in square units.

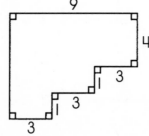

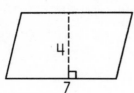

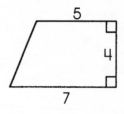

1. _____

2. _____

3. _____

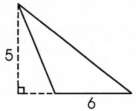

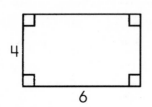

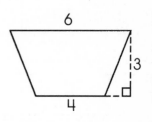

4. _____

5. _____

6. _____

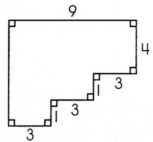

7. _____

8. _____

Name _____

Fill Me Up

To find the volume of the sculpture, first find the volume of each three-dimensional shape. Add each total together to find a total volume. Remember to use the same measurements for similar shapes.   V = l • w • h

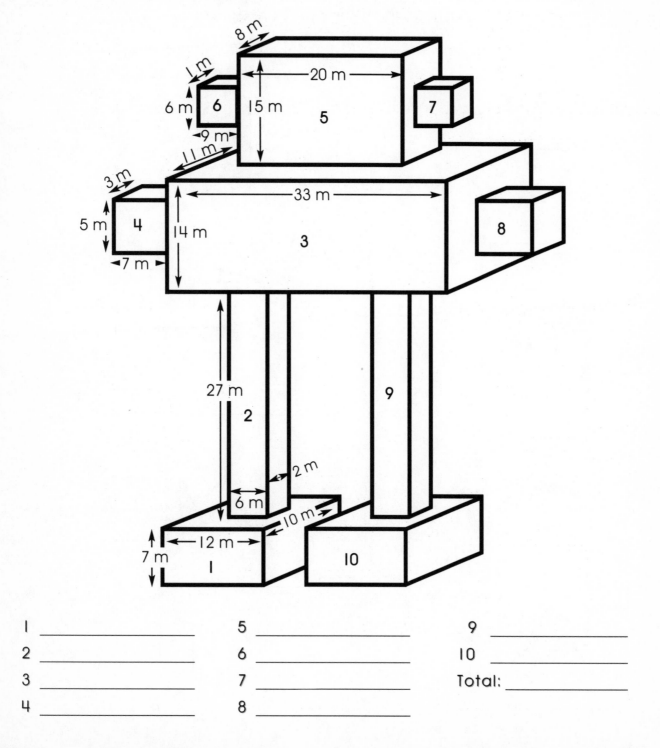

1 _____	5 _____	9 _____
2 _____	6 _____	10 _____
3 _____	7 _____	Total: _____
4 _____	8 _____	

Name _____

Prisms

Volume = area of base x height

Find the volume of the following prisms. The bases are shaded.

1. _____

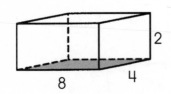

8   4   2

2. _____

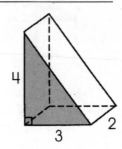

4   3   2

3. _____

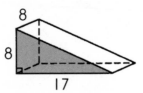

8
8
17

4. _____

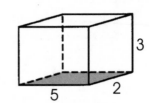

3
5   2

5. _____

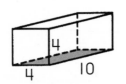

4
4   10

6. _____

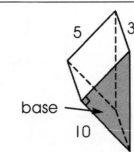

5   3

base
10

7. _____

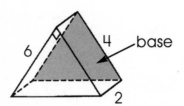

6   4   base
2

8. _____

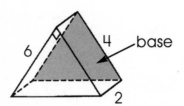

3
3   3

Name _____

Conversions

The stunt bike club had a tournament to see who could do the longest jump. Convert the measurement of each leap below.

1 foot (ft.)	=	12 inches (in.)
1 yard (yd.)	=	3 feet (ft.)
1 yard (yd.)	=	36 inches (in.)

1. 24 ft. _____ yd.

2. 7 ft. _____ in.

3. 96 in. _____ ft.

4. 20 ft. _____ in.

5. 3 yd. _____ ft.

6. 12 ft. _____ in.

7. 15 ft. _____ yd.

8. 2 yd. _____ in.

9. 12 ft. _____ yd.

10. 4 yd. _____ ft.

11. 24 in. _____ ft.

12. 18 ft. _____ yd.

13. 36 in. _____ ft.

14. Order the converted lengths from least to greatest to see who won the competition.

_____

_____

_____

Popping Puzzler

Use the facts in the conversion box to match the unit equivalents by drawing a line.
Then, write the word next to each answer on the correct blank line below.

1 pound (lb.) =	16 ounces (oz.)
1 ton (t.) =	2,000 pounds (lb.)
1 ton (t.) =	32,000 ounces (oz.)

1. 210 lb.   160,000 oz.   better

2. 8,000 lb.   6 t.   and

3. 64 oz.   5,616 oz.   with

4. 10,000 lb.   4 t.   tastes

5. 351 lb.   4 lb.   even

6. 15 t.   11 lb.   salt

7. 12,000 lb.   3,360 oz.   Popcorn

8. 176 oz.   30,000 lb.   butter

_____   _____   _____   _____
     1   2   3   4

_____   _____   _____   _____ .
     5   6   7   8

Select an appropriate unit for weighing each of the following—ounce, pound, or ton.

9.   a leaf   _____

10. an orange   _____

11. a refrigerator _____

12. a moving van   _____

13. a bag of sugar _____

14. a sailboat   _____

Note The Units of Capacity

Study the notes and the capacity box to complete the problems.

To change from a larger unit to a smaller unit, multiply.
To change from a smaller unit to a larger unit, divide.

1 cup (c.) =	8 fluid ounces (fl. oz.)
1 pint (pt.) =	2 cups (c.)
1 quart (qt.) =	2 pints (pt.)
1 gallon (gal.) =	4 quarts (qt.)

Convert each measurement to the unit given.

1. 8 pt. = _____ c.

2. 48 fl. oz. = _____ c.

3. 12 pt. = _____ fl. oz.

4. 2 gal. = _____ pt.

5. 27 c. = _____ pt.

6. 320 fl. oz. = _____ pt.

7. 14 qt. = _____ pt.

8. 3 gal. = _____ qt.

9. 24 pt. = _____ qt.

Compare using <, >, or =.

10. 24 fl. oz. _____ 3 c.

11. 26 c. _____ 208 fl. oz.

12. 8 pt. _____ 28 c.

13. 12 qt. _____ 20 pt.

14. 23 gal. _____ 23 qt.

15. 8 qt. _____ 8 gal.

Name _____

It's Hot and Cold Outside

Study the following recorded temperatures for eight different scenarios and list the correct temperatures.

Average Cold Day
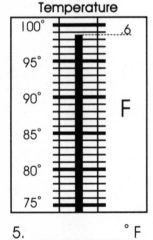

1. _____ °F

Cold Michigan Day
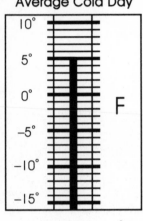

2. _____ °F

Freezing Point
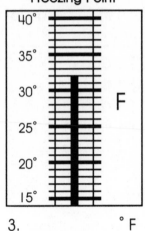

3. _____ °F

Average Chilly Day
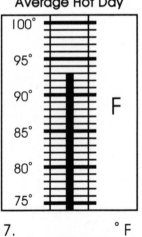

4. _____ °F

Normal Body Temperature
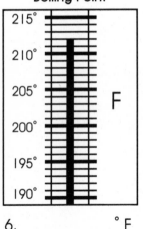

5. _____ °F

Boiling Point
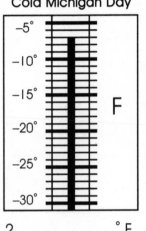

6. _____ °F

Average Hot Day
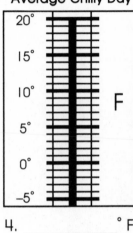

7. _____ °F

Hot Day In Las Vegas
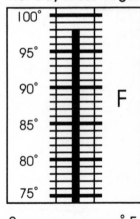

8. _____ °F

9. List the number of days above that water would remain frozen. _____

10. How many degrees difference is there between the freezing point and the boiling point? _____

11. How many more degrees is the boiling point than the hot day in Las Vegas? _____

12. How many degrees different is the freezing point than a cold day in Michigan? _____

13. What is the difference in degrees between our body temperature and an average hot day? _____

Name _____

Measuring Metrics

Match each amount on the left to its equivalent amount on the right by drawing a line.

I meter (m) =	100 centimeters (cm)
I meter (m) =	1,000 millimeters (mm)
I centimeter (cm) =	10 millimeters (mm)

1. 40 m   5,000 mm

2. 16 m   60,000 mm

3. 2,400 cm   12,000 mm

4. 60 m   4,000 cm

5. 32 m   16,000 mm

6. 7 m   24 m

7. 500 cm   3,200 cm

8. 12 m   700 cm

Complete the equations.

9. ____ mm = 2 m   10. I cm = ____ mm

11. 20 mm = ____ cm   12. ____ m = 5,000 mm

13. ____ cm = 2.5 m   14. 15 cm = ____ m

15. 2 cm = ____ mm   16. 4 m = ____ cm

Answer the following word problems.

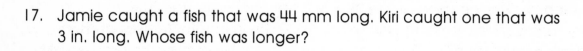

17. Jamie caught a fish that was 44 mm long. Kiri caught one that was 3 in. long. Whose fish was longer?

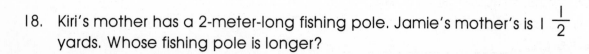

18. Kiri's mother has a 2-meter-long fishing pole. Jamie's mother's is $1\frac{1}{2}$ yards. Whose fishing pole is longer?

Name _____

Here's a Challenge for You

Think about each problem. Diagram or write out the problem and then solve it.

1. Sam just realized that each slice of the bread that he purchased at the store
    for his parents is 1 cm in width. Each loaf contains 25 slices. If the total width of
    the loaves is 100 cm, how many loaves are there? How many meters does that
    total in all? _____

2. Kamal's father is laying brick to build a barbeque. Each brick is 5 cm in length.
    He is leaving a 1 cm width of mortar between each brick. How many bricks will
    he lay before he reaches a height of 23 cm? (Note: height does not include
    mortar on the top brick.) _____

3. Saeed would like to space six 25 cm-wide chairs across the front porch. He
    wants to leave 10 cm between each chair. The porch is 2 m and 20 cm wide.
    Will he have enough room for his guests? If he sets out 3 rows of 6 chairs in
    each, how many chairs will that be in all? _____

4. Mark's golden retriever ran forward 600 cm, then back 100 cm, then forward
    200 cm, in order to catch the flying disk in the air. How many meters did the
    dog actually move forward? _____

5. Three subs were purchased for the picnic that the fifth grade class was having
    to celebrate the opening of the new school. Each sub was 200 cm in length.
    At the end of the picnic, the first sub was 30 cm in length, the second was
    50 cm in length, and the third was 40 cm in length. Did they have a total of
    more or less than 1 meter remaining of sub sandwich to munch on? If so, how
    much more or less than a meter did they have remaining? _____

On the Move with Metric Units

Study the conversion box and look at the objects pictured. Try to determine what weight each would logically be: **milligrams**, **grams**, or **kilograms.**

1. 5 _____

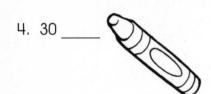

2. 40 _____

1,000 milligram (mg) =	1 gram (g)
1,000 (g) =	1 kilogram (kg)
1,000 (kg) =	1 metric ton (t)

3. 4 _____

4. 30 _____

5. 25 _____

6. 3 _____

7. 4 _____

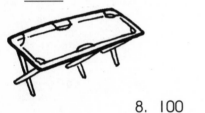

8. 100 _____

9. 125 _____

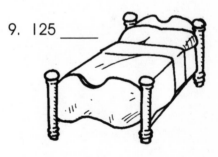

10. 225 _____

11. 2 _____

Complete the following equations.

12. _____ mg = 2 g

13. 3,000 g = _____ kg

14. 25,000,000 mg = _____ kg

15. 5,000 kg = _____ t

16. _____ kg = 6 t

17. 2 kg = _____ g

18. 4.5 t = _____ kg

19. _____ kg = 36,000,000 mg

Rotational Rhetoric

The rotation of the earth on its 23° axis produces night and day. Do you know how fast the earth is rotating? To find out, match the kilogram amounts in the key with the gram amounts below each blank. Then fill in the blanks with the coordinating letters.

```
Key:
D = 5 kg      G = 2 kg      M = 8 kg
E = 11 kg     H = 15 kg     L = 25 kg
R = 50 kg     I = 6 kg      P = 7 kg
T = 1 kg      O = 3 kg      A = 9 kg
S = 75 kg     N = 4 kg      U = 10 kg
```

___ ___   ___ ___
6,000 g 1,000 g   6,000 g 75,000 g

___ ___ ___ ___ ___ ___ ___ ___
50,000 g 3,000 g 1,000 g 9,000 g 1,000 g 6,000 g 4,000 g 2,000 g

___ ___   ___ ___ ___
9,000 g 1,000 g   3,000 g 4,000 g 11,000 g

___ ___ ___ ___ ___ ___ ___ ___
1,000 g 15,000 g 3,000 g 10,000 g 75,000 g 9,000 g 4,000 g 5,000 g

___ ___ ___ ___ ___
8,000 g 6,000 g 25,000 g 11,000 g 75,000 g

___ ___ ___   ___ ___ ___ ___!
7,000 g 11,000 g 50,000 g   15,000 g 3,000 g 10,000 g 50,000 g

Name _____

Unbelievable Units of Capacity

Match each picture with the correct capacity. Then place the matching letter on the correct blank below to answer the question.

1.   T.   20 L

2.   C.   4 L

3.   E.   900 L

4.   R.   250 mL

5.   I.   1 L

6.   M.   100 L

What kinds of units of capacity are these?

___   ___   ___   ___   ___   ___
 4   1   6   2   5   3

Circle the correct metric unit.

7.   Sorcha helped milk her grandpa's cow. She filled a bucket with 6 (mL, L) of milk.

8.   For breakfast, Feroz drank 300 (mL, L) of orange juice.

9.   Monica's dad used 35 (mL, L) of paint to paint the outside of their garage and their doghouse.

10.   Felix filled his aquarium with 20 (mL, L) of water.

11.   Mary helped her mom fill their punch bowl with 3 (mL, L) of punch.

Crossword Conversions

Complete the crossword puzzle below with number words after you convert the milliliter clues to liters. The first one is done for you.

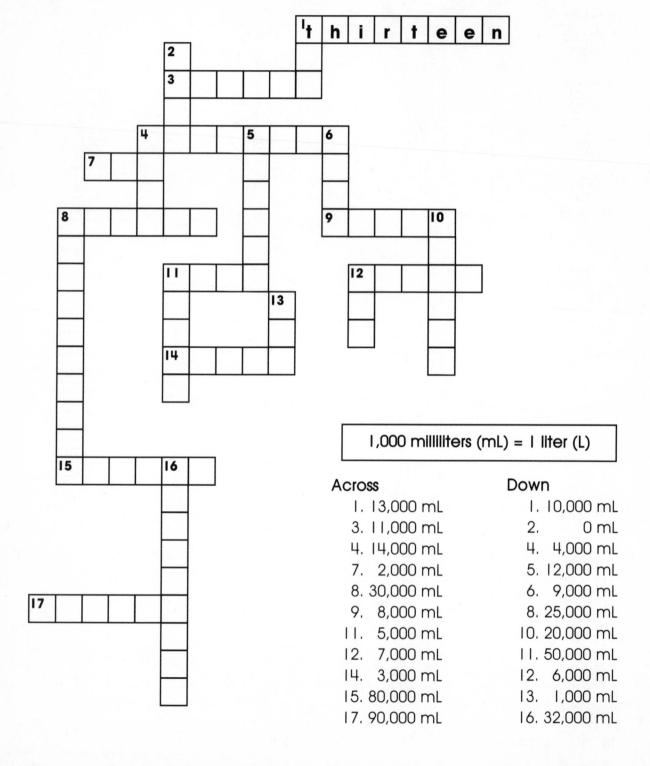

1,000 milliliters (mL) = 1 liter (L)

Across

1. 13,000 mL
3. 11,000 mL
4. 14,000 mL
7. 2,000 mL
8. 30,000 mL
9. 8,000 mL
11. 5,000 mL
12. 7,000 mL
14. 3,000 mL
15. 80,000 mL
17. 90,000 mL

Down

1. 10,000 mL
2.   0 mL
4. 4,000 mL
5. 12,000 mL
6. 9,000 mL
8. 25,000 mL
10. 20,000 mL
11. 50,000 mL
12. 6,000 mL
13. 1,000 mL
16. 32,000 mL

Name _____

Sensational Celsius

Study the thermometers and record the correct temperature.

Freezing Point

Normal Body Temperature

Boiling Point

Refrigerator

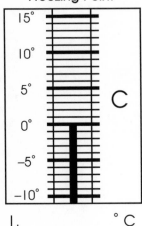 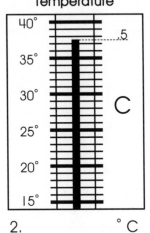 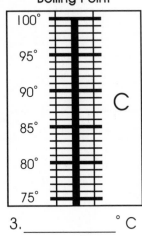 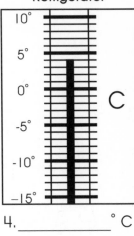

1. _____ °C   2. _____ °C   3. _____ °C   4. _____ °C

Shade in the correct temperatures.

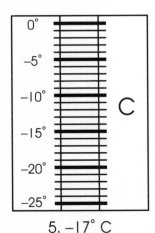 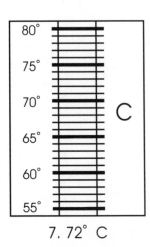 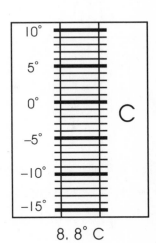

5. –17° C   6. 44° C   7. 72° C   8. 8° C

9. What is the difference in degrees between the boiling point of water and our normal body temperature? _____

10. What is the boiling point of water in Celsius? At what degree does water boil in Fahrenheit? _____

_____

11. What is the difference between the temperature in the refrigerator and the freezing point? _____

12. What is the freezing point of water in Celsius? At what degree does water freeze in Fahrenheit?

_____

_____

Name _____

Calculator Conversions

Figure how many kilometers it takes to equal the following distances in miles.

$$\boxed{1 \text{ mi.} = 1.6 \text{ km}}$$

1. 3 mi. = _____ km

2. 5 mi. = _____ km

3. 10 mi. = _____ km

4. 2 mi. = _____ km

5. 6 mi. = _____ km

6. 4 mi. = _____ km

7. 9 mi. = _____ km

8. 7 mi. = _____ km

9. 12 mi. = _____ km

10. 25 mi. = _____ km

11. 15 mi. = _____ km

12. 8 mi. = _____ km

13. 1 mi. = _____ km

14. 0.5 mi. = _____ km

Name _____

How Do They Compare?

Convert pounds below to kilograms. Use this formula to find equivalent amounts. Round to the nearest tenth.

| Pound weight ÷ 2.2 = equivalent kilogram mass |

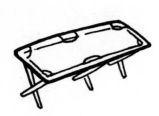

1. 12 lb. = _____ kg   2. 5 lb. = _____ kg   3. 210 lb. = _____ kg

4. 80 lb. = _____ kg   5. 25 lb. = _____ kg   6. 10 lb. = _____ kg

7. 50 lb. = _____ kg   8. 2.2 lb. = _____ kg   9. 11 lb. = _____ kg

       IF87127 *Standards-Based Math*

Name _____

Does It Measure Up?

To follow recipes, you need to know how to measure ingredients. The bakery has just published a cookie cookbook that included chocolate chip cookies. There's only one problem; the recipe needs to be converted to metric. Look at the table and convert the recipe.

Conversion Table		
1 cup	=	240 milliliters (mL)
$\frac{2}{3}$ cup	=	160 milliliters (mL)
$\frac{1}{2}$ cup	=	120 milliliters (mL)
$\frac{1}{4}$ cup	=	60 milliliters (mL)
1 tbsp.	=	15 milliliters (mL)
1 tsp.	=	5 milliliters (mL)

$2\frac{1}{4}$ cups flour =   _____ mL

2 cups white sugar =   _____ mL

$\frac{2}{3}$ cup brown sugar =   _____ mL

$1\frac{1}{2}$ tsp. vanilla =   _____ mL

$1\frac{1}{2}$ tbsp. baking soda =   _____ mL

$1\frac{1}{2}$ cups butter =   _____ mL

$\frac{1}{2}$ tsp. salt =   _____ mL

2 eggs =   _____ eggs

$2\frac{1}{2}$ cups chocolate chips =   _____ mL

Name _____

A Cold Day

Look at the table below that shows temperatures for a cold day in January. Plot the information as a line graph below.

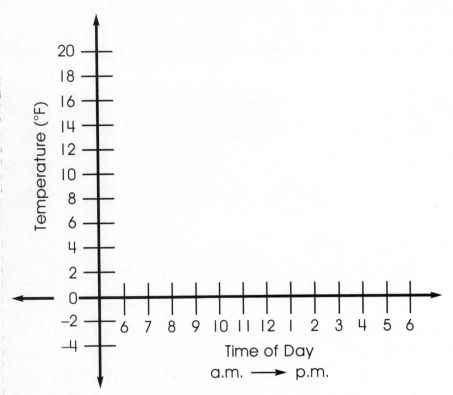

Time	Temp. (°F)
6 a.m.	−2
7 a.m.	−2
8 a.m.	−1
9 a.m.	2
10 a.m.	5
11 a.m.	8
12 p.m.	12
1 p.m.	14
2 p.m.	13
3 p.m.	15
4 p.m.	12
5 p.m.	11
6 p.m.	9

1. Which is easier to read, the table or the graph? _____

   Why? _____

   _____

   _____

2. What general statement can you make about the results of the graph?

   _____

   _____

   _____

   _____

Name _____

The Right Questions

Write a question about each set of information and then answer it.

1. A 12-piece tub of crispy chicken and a side of mashed potatoes costs $18.95. Nina and her family share the chicken dinner every time they go to Chicken Little Restaurant. They ate at the restaurant 4 times in the month of April.

   _____

   _____

2. Eight hundred seventy people went to the restaurant in 1 week. One thousand, seven hundred and forty went in 2 weeks.

   _____

   _____

3. The restaurant has 19 tables with 6 chairs at each table.

   _____

   _____

4. Nina and her friends, Anthea and Maya, spent $7.40 on a chicken sandwich, a soda, and a slice of pie. They shared the cost equally.

   _____

   _____

5. At the restaurant, the owner said it takes 20 minutes to make coleslaw and potatoes to go with the chicken dinners, 60 minutes to open the restaurant, and 30 minutes to close up.

   _____

   _____

6. The restaurant offers 6 different soups each week. There are 52 weeks in a year.

   _____

7. Nina and her friend Anthea went to the restaurant with $25.00. They spent $14.90.

   _____

   _____

Ducky Data

Raquel's science class at school helped the town's wetland club capture and tag ducks for research. Study the data collected to answer the questions below.

Week	no. of ducks captured	no. of ducks tagged	% of ducks tagged
1	25	2	_____
2	40	4	_____
3	60	6	_____
4	20	8	_____

1. What percentage of the ducks were tagged during Week 1? _____

2. Which week had the least amount of ducks tagged according to the number of ducks captured? _____

3. How many ducks were captured in total? _____

4. Does there seem to be a pattern between the weeks and the number of ducks tagged? If so, what is it? _____

   _____

   _____

5. If Week 5 had 112 ducks captured, how many, according to the pattern, would you predict would have been tagged in that week? Explain your answer. _____

   _____

   _____

Graph It

Use the following information to complete the circle graphs.

1. Birthplaces of the first ten
   U.S. presidents:

Virginia	60%
Massachusetts	20%
New York	10%
South Carolina	10%

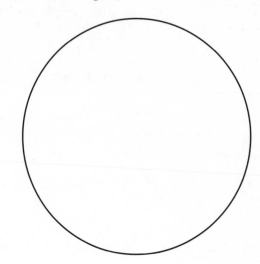

2. Trash collected on Earth Day:

paper	50%
aluminum cans	15%
plastic	15%
rubber	10%
glass	10%

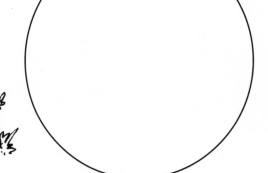

3. Pizza preferences:

cheese	30%
cheese/pepperoni	20%
cheese/mushroom	10%
deluxe	40%

Name _____

Double Up

Continual Time Without Rest at Swim Team Workouts

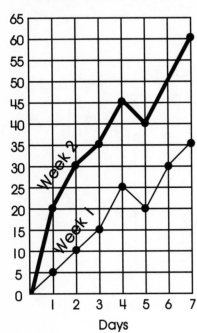

1. On the very first day of workouts, how soon after Mary started did she need to take a rest?

   _____

2. In week 1, how soon did Mary need to rest on day number 3?

   _____

3. How long could she go without rest on the third day of the second week?

   _____

4. What is the range of week 1? _____

5. What is the range of week 2? _____

6. Did Mary improve in both weeks?

   _____

7. Which class received 18 letters more often within a 1-month period?

   _____

8. Which class received the most letters in the first month?

   _____

Overseas Letters Received from France

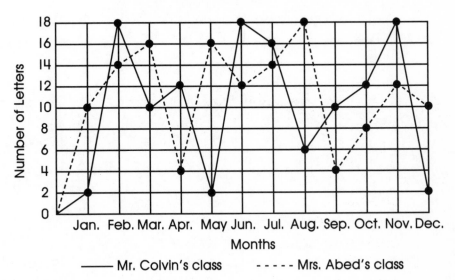

——— Mr. Colvin's class   - - - - - Mrs. Abed's class

9. How many letters did Mrs. Abed's class receive in all? _____

10. Which class received more letters? _____

11. Which class only received 2 letters in January, May, and December?

_____

Comparing Data

A double bar graph allows more than one set of data to be compared. The following double bar graph compares the growth between two states (rounded to the nearest half million).

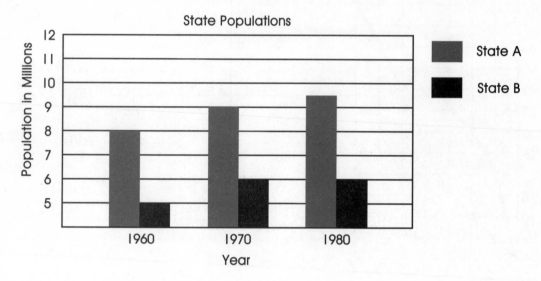

Use the double bar graph above to answer the following questions.

1. What was the population of State A in 1960?

   _____

2. What was the growth of State A from 1960 to 1970?

   _____

3. What was the population of State B in 1960?

   _____

4. What was State B's population gain from 1960 to 1970?

   _____

5. Which state experienced the greatest growth in population from 1970 to 1980?

   _____

6. Which state had the greatest population growth from 1960 to 1980? What was it?

   _____

Taking a Survey

A city is considering a proposal to build a new shopping mall within the city boundaries. Before it is put to a vote, the mayor decides to take a survey. Out of 4,250 residents and 182 local businesses, 1,000 people were surveyed. The results are graphed below.

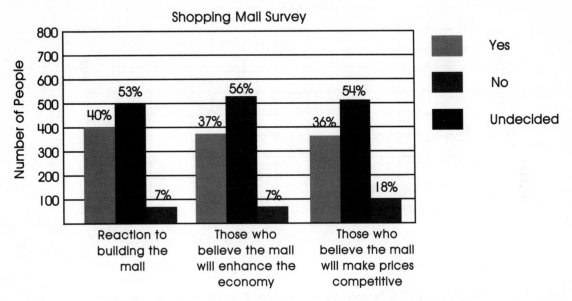

Based on the information in the graph, answer the following questions.

1. Should the mall be built? _____
    Explain. _____

    _____

2. Give two reasons why the city council should vote in favor of the shopping
    mall proposal. _____

    _____

3. Give two reasons why the city council should vote against the shopping mall
    proposal. _____

    _____

4. What is the mean of the percentage of people who voted yes on the three
    questions? _____

Graphs

Graphs have a vertical and a horizontal axis. The axes are labeled to show what is being compared.

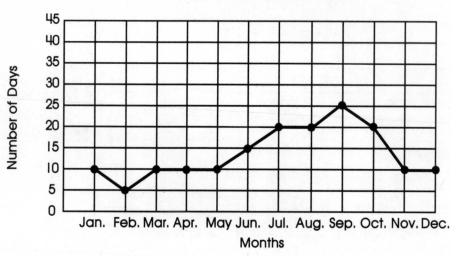

Average Number of Rainy Days

Use the line graph above to answer the following questions.

1. What is the title of the graph?

   _____

2. How is the vertical axis labeled?

   _____

3. What is contained in the horizontal axis?

   _____

4. Which month had the greatest number of rainy days?

   _____

5. Which 2-month period shows the greatest change in the number of rainy days?

   _____

6. Which month was the driest?

   _____

7. Based on this graph, which month should have been the best for tourists? Explain.

   _____

   _____

   _____

Using the graph, fill in the blanks below.

8. range: _____

9. mean: _____

10. mode _____

Name _____

Family Income

Use the graph about the Oren family income for one year to answer the questions below.

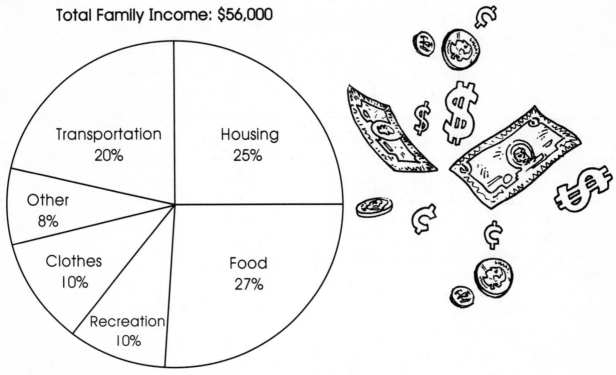

Total Family Income: $56,000

Transportation 20%
Housing 25%
Other 8%
Clothes 10%
Food 27%
Recreation 10%

1. How much money is spent on recreation per year?

    _____

2. Does the Oren family spend more on Clothes, Recreation, and Other than it does on Housing?

    _____

3. On what does the family spend most of its money? _____

4. How much money is spent on food? _____

5. If the family income were increased by $10,000, how much more would they be able to spend on Clothes?

    _____

6. Given a $10,000 increase, what then would be the total amount of money spent on Recreation?

    _____

Name _____

Finding Averages

Find the mean, median, mode, and range of each set of data below.

Mile Relay Practice Times	
Day	*Time (minutes)*
Monday	3.29
Tuesday	3.24
Wednesday	3.48
Thursday	3.24
Friday	3.89

1. Mean: _____

   Median: _____

   Mode: _____

   Range: _____

Candy Bars Sold	
Day	*Number of Bars*
Monday	127
Tuesday	225
Wednesday	93
Thursday	82
Friday	111
Saturday	137
Sunday	82

2. Mean: _____

   Median: _____

   Mode: _____

   Range: _____

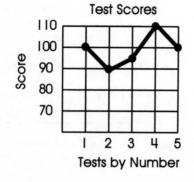

3. Mean: _____

   Median: _____

   Mode: _____

   Range: _____

What's the Vote?

Alyson's class is interested in growing a flower garden for the whole school to enjoy. To collect data on flower preferences, they surveyed the students in the school. Out of an enrollment of 435, the following resulted.

Favorite Flowers

Type of Flower	Number of Votes
Black-Eyed Susan	57
Lavender	63
Iris	32
Tulip	78
Hollyhock	7
Daffodil	53
Daisy	84

1. List the flowers in order from the least popular to the most.

   _____

   _____

   _____

2. Based on the data, which 5 flowers should the class plant?

   _____

   _____

3. Which flower should definitely not be planted? _____

4. Do the number of votes justify planting a garden? _____

   Why? _____

   _____

   _____

5. What is the mean? _____

6. What is the mode? _____

7. What is the median? _____

8. What is the range? _____

Diagramming

Look at the tree diagram below. Name all the outcomes.

1.

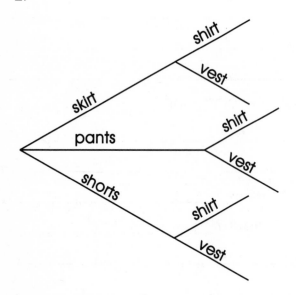

a. _____
b. _____
c. _____
d. _____
e. _____
f. _____

2.

a. _____
b. _____
c. _____
d. _____
e. _____
f. _____

3. Use the back of this paper to draw a tree diagram for the description below.
    The food is hot or cold. It tastes sweet, salty, or tangy.

Predicting Outcomes

To find the probability of an outcome, we must find the relative frequency of that outcome. This can be expressed as a ratio:

$$\frac{\text{frequency of outcome}}{\text{total frequency of all outcomes}}$$

We can also use this equation to predict future outcomes. Simply make an equality with n (the frequency) as an unknown number.

For example, if $\frac{12}{50}$ is the probability of having a rainy day out of 50 days, then $\frac{n}{100}$ might be the prediction of having n amount of rainy days out of 100 days.

$$\frac{12}{50} = \frac{n}{100}$$

$$n = 24$$

1. If the probability of having rain is $\frac{8}{50}$, meaning that rain had fallen 8 out of the last 50 days, how many days would you expect it to rain out of the next 100?

    _____

2. Explain why using probability may or may not be a good way to predict the weather. _____

    _____

    _____

3. If 32 out of 36 students pick red as their favorite color, what could you assume about the results of a sampling of 108 students?

    _____

    _____

Playing Games

Solve the probability problems below.

1. A jar contains 4 blue marbles, 8 red marbles, 2 yellow marbles, and 12 orange marbles. Find the probability of:

    a. P (red or blue marble)   _____

    b. P (orange marble)   _____

    c. P (yellow or orange marble)   _____

    d. P (a marble)   _____

    e. P (a green marble)   _____

2. Marty and Chandra have played jacks during recess 18 out of the last 30 days. What is the probability that they will play jacks today?

    _____

3. During indoor recess, Leah, Shalti, and Benny were allowed to play with either the pogo stick, the yo-yo, or the jump rope. In how many different ways can the students be matched to the toys? List them. _____

    _____

    _____

4. Fifty students were surveyed. Forty preferred soccer to four-square. Predict how many students out of 200 would prefer soccer.

    _____

5. For being star of the week, Justin may choose to play either jacks, go-fish, or solitaire, and he may choose a snack of popcorn or pretzels. What is the probability he will choose jacks and popcorn?_____

Answer Key

1. 7   2. 9   3. 3   4. 8
5. 5   6. 6   7. 4   8. 3
9. b   10. d   11. c   12. a
13. Possible answers include: 240.1323; 240.1423; 240.1523; 240.1623; 240.1723; 240.1823; 240.1923; 241.1323; 241.1423; 241.1523; 241.1623; 241.1723; 241.1823; 241.1923
14. 0.54123

1. thirty thousand, six hundred twenty-one
2. 30,000,000 + 1,000,000 + 300,000 + 80,000 + 9,000 + 200 + 50
3. 26,618,567
4. spider
5. ant and earwig
6. 72,794,500; 70,000,000 + 2,000,000 + 700,000 + 90,000 + 4,000 + 500; seventy-two million, seven hundred ninety-four thousand, five hundred

1. 10,000 + 1,000 + 700 + 60 + 3
2. 9,000 + 600 + 50 + 1
3. 20,000 + 5,000 + 300 + 40 + 1
4. 700 + 40 + 2
5. 2,000 + 900 + 60 + 2
6. 32,950
7. 11,111
8. 6,499
9. 558
10. 8,186
11. twenty-three million, forty-two thousand, three hundred sixty-eight
12. forty-eight million, two
13. two billion, five hundred thousand
14. four million, twenty thousand

1. $^-2$ 2. 1   3. $^-4$ 4. $^-2$
5. 1   6. 3   7. $^-9$ 8. 2
9. 3   10. $^-7$

1. 41   2. $^-65$ 3. $^-261$ 4. $^-171$
5. 81   6. $^-57$ 7. $^-65$ 8. 30
9. $^-12$ 10. $^-128$ 11. $^-1$ 12. $^-21$
13. 47   14. $^-51$ 15. 59   16. 144
17. 1   18. $^-5$ 19. 12   20. 0
21. 24   22. $^-127$

1. 2   2. 29   3. 7   4. 22
5. $^-53$ 6. 50   7. $^-17$ 8. $^-14$
9. 9   10. 63   11. $^-51$ 12. 47
A = ($^-2$, 8)   B = ($^-9$, 2)   C ($^-16$, $^-4$)
D = ($^-14$, $^-5$)   E = ($^-11$, $^-2$)   F = ($^-8$, $^-4$)
G = ($^-5$, $^-2$)   H = ($^-2$, $^-4$)   I = (1, $^-2$)
J = (4, $^-4$)   K = (7, $^-2$)   L = (10, $^-5$)
M = (12, $^-4$)   N = (5, 2)

1. =   2. >   3. <   4. <
5. >   6. =   7. =   8. =
9. =   10. >   11. >   12. =
13. <   14. <   15. <   16. =
17.–18. Answers will vary.

$^{36}\!/_{60}$ = $^3\!/_5$

Yes

1. $^5\!/_{13}$ 2. $^3\!/_7$ 3. $^1\!/_4$ 4. $^5\!/_{19}$
5. $^2\!/_3$ 6. $^3\!/_{17}$ 7. $^1\!/_{14}$ 8. $^3\!/_{11}$
9. $^4\!/_7$ 10. $^7\!/_8$ 11. $^{18}\!/_{32}$ 12. $^2\!/_3$
13. $^{14}\!/_{63}$ 14. $^{15}\!/_{25}$

1. 13 $^2\!/_3$ 2. 1 $^{24}\!/_{31}$ 3. 1 $^7\!/_{19}$
4. 13 $^4\!/_9$ 5. 1 $^1\!/_{25}$ 6. 18 $^5\!/_6$
7. 4 $^5\!/_8$ 8. 46½   9. 1
10. 21 $^1\!/_3$ 11. $^7\!/_6$ = 1 $^1\!/_6$ 12. $^5\!/_2$ = 2 ½
13. $^7\!/_4$ = 1 $^3\!/_4$
Number 9 is circled.

1. 3 $^9\!/_{13}$ 2. 2 $^4\!/_5$ 3. 5 $^3\!/_4$ 4. 6 $^3\!/_5$
5. 35½   6. 4 $^4\!/_7$ 7. 9 $^5\!/_6$ 8. 7 $^1\!/_3$
9. 11 $^3\!/_4$ 10. 6 $^5\!/_6$ 11. 31   12. 2

1. 2   2. 1 $^1\!/_9$ 3. 1 $^1\!/_{24}$ 4. $^{19}\!/_{42}$
5. 1 $^{11}\!/_{30}$ 6. $^{13}\!/_{15}$ 7. $^3\!/_4$ 8. $^{37}\!/_{40}$
9. $^3\!/_{40}$ 10. $^{14}\!/_{15}$ 11. $^{11}\!/_{30}$ 12. 1 $^{11}\!/_{24}$

Left to right, top to bottom: 1, $^{13}\!/_{18}$, $^5\!/_6$, 1 $^1\!/_{18}$, $^1\!/_3$, $^{14}\!/_{15}$, 1 $^7\!/_{16}$, 1 $^{19}\!/_{40}$, 1 $^{29}\!/_{40}$, $^{13}\!/_{16}$

What's the Difference? ....page 19

1. $\frac{1}{8}$ 2. $\frac{14}{99}$ 3. $\frac{1}{9}$ 4. $\frac{16}{35}$
5. $\frac{1}{63}$ 6. $\frac{5}{36}$ 7. $\frac{5}{8}$ 8. $\frac{11}{36}$
9. $\frac{1}{30}$ 10. $\frac{2}{3}$ 11. $\frac{11}{15}$ 12. $\frac{1}{10}$
13. $\frac{1}{4}, \frac{3}{8}, \frac{5}{12}$; sum—$\frac{2}{3}$; diff.—$\frac{1}{6}$
14. $\frac{3}{10}, \frac{3}{4}, \frac{4}{5}, \frac{7}{8}$; sum—$1\frac{7}{40}$; diff.—$\frac{23}{40}$

Seawater Solutions ....page 20

1. $\frac{2}{5}$ 2. $\frac{3}{10}$ 3. $\frac{1}{3}$ 4. $\frac{1}{5}$
5. $\frac{9}{20}$ 6. $\frac{1}{10}$ 7. $\frac{1}{2}$ 8. $\frac{19}{33}$
Moby Pickle
9. $\frac{14}{19}$ 10. $\frac{5}{8}$ 11. $\frac{41}{30}$ 12. $\frac{13}{25}$
13. $\frac{3}{16}$ or $\frac{1}{4}$ 14. $\frac{5}{8}$

Cycling for Fractions ....page 21

1. $\frac{3}{4}$ 2. $\frac{1}{4}$ 3. $\frac{3}{4}$ 4. $\frac{4}{12}$
5. $\frac{8}{12}$ 6. $\frac{2}{12}$ 7. $\frac{10}{12}$ 8. $\frac{9}{12}$
9. $\frac{38}{36}$ 10. $\frac{11}{36}$ 11. $\frac{17}{36}$ 12. $\frac{5}{36}$
13. $\frac{14}{36}$ 14. $\frac{2}{36}$ 15. $\frac{20}{36} = \frac{5}{9}$

Piece It Together ....page 22

1. $5\frac{1}{3}$ 2. $23\frac{1}{3}$ 3. $1\frac{1}{2}$ 4. $\frac{2}{3}$
5. $2\frac{17}{20}$ 6. $1\frac{1}{5}$ 7. $\frac{1}{8}$ 8. $\frac{1}{18}$
9. $2\frac{1}{7}$ 10. $\frac{10}{21}$ 11. $2\frac{3}{5}$ 12. $\frac{5}{12}$
13. 2 14. $\frac{8}{15}$ 15. $5\frac{5}{6}$ 16. 25 lb.
17. $\frac{3}{8}$

Climbing Pyramids ....page 23
Read from bottom:
Pyramid 1: $1, 3, \frac{2}{3}, \frac{1}{4}, \frac{1}{3}, 4\frac{1}{2}, 2\frac{2}{3}, \frac{2}{27}, 1\frac{11}{16}, \frac{32}{729}$
Pyramid 2: $\frac{1}{6}, \frac{1}{4}, \frac{1}{3}, \frac{2}{15}, \frac{1}{24}, \frac{1}{12}, \frac{2}{45}, \frac{1}{288}, \frac{1}{270}, \frac{1}{77,760}$

Mix It Up ....page 24

1. $7\frac{1}{12}$ 2. $7\frac{13}{18}$ 3. $4\frac{1}{5}$ 4. $10\frac{7}{24}$
5. $\frac{9}{10}$ 6. $1\frac{3}{5}$ 7. $4\frac{7}{9}$ 8. $5\frac{11}{15}$
9. $5\frac{1}{20}$ 10. $1\frac{5}{18}$ 11. $10\frac{1}{8}$ 12. 3
13. $3\frac{31}{72}$ 14. $13\frac{2}{3}$ 15. $11\frac{1}{3}$ 16. $11\frac{4}{15}$

All Mixed Up ....page 25

1. $2\frac{1}{4}$ 2. 5 3. $7\frac{1}{2}$ 4. $7\frac{1}{5}$
5. $6\frac{7}{8}$ 6. $1\frac{2}{3}$ 7. $7\frac{7}{9}$ 8. $1\frac{23}{28}$
9. $11\frac{3}{7}$ 10. $7\frac{5}{7}$ 11. $\frac{19}{28}$ 12. $2\frac{3}{5}$

Estimate Me ....page 26

1. 72; 87.6035   2. 320; 323.0433   3. 182; 185.844
4. 210; 214.446   5. 528; 529.2406   6. 120; 119.961
7. 114; 120.9329   8. 48; 53.613   9. 332; 314.374
10. 164; 170.154

Traveling ....page 27

1. 31.0   2. 28.25   3. 32.86
4. 23.25   5. 27.14   6. 27.09
7. 48.14   8. 48.11   9. 51.13
10. 48.32   11. 51.02   12. 18.41
13. 32.66   14. 26.57   15. 36

Gift-Wrapped Decimals ....page 28

1. 202 sq. in.   2. 1,015.28 sq. in.   3. 269.98 sq.in.
4. 68.5 sq. in.   5. 154.14 sq. in.   6. 630.46 sq. in.
7. 121.5 sq. in.
Grand Total: 2,461.86 sq. in.

Write It Out ....page 29

1. 6.16   2. 29.23
3. 0.8325   4. 3.21
5. 15.75 grams   6. 109.72 calories
7. 45.9 grams

Animal Trivia ....page 30

1. 17.25   2. 3.52
3. 7.1   4. 66.76
5. 53.33   6. 133.33
Tongue

1. 3.545   2. 56.94
3. 61.1   4. 19.207
5. 7.02   6. 0.252
7. 0.0357   8. 83.4
Ten Miles

Nothing Corny ....page 31

1. 0.156   2. 0.01   3. 71.9   4. 38.412
5. 33.3   6. 257.6   7. 54.1   8. 99.4
9. 36.5   10. 29.2   11. 222.2   12. 21.5
13. 0.24   14. 0.654   15. 4.005
16. Flour corn—$4.50/bushel

Point the Way ....page 32

1. 0.25   2. 0.3   3. 0.1   4. 0.5
5. 0.5   6. 0.0625   7. 0.75   8. 0.2
9. 0.06   10. 0.1   11. 0.2   12. 0.0125

Delicious Decimals ....page 33
0.25 cup parsley
0.25 cup basil
0.5 tablespoon vinegar
2 cups tomato sauce
0.125 teaspoon garlic
0.75 teaspoon salt
0.25 tablespoon chili powder
0.33 cup chopped mushrooms
0.5 cup green peppers
1 cup meatballs

Abstract Art ....page 34
Designs will vary.

Color	Fraction	Decimal	Percent	Number
Blue	$\frac{14}{100}$	0.14	14%	14
Purple	$\frac{8}{100}$	0.08	8%	8
Red	$\frac{12}{100}$	0.12	12%	12
Yellow	$\frac{26}{100}$	0.26	26%	26
Green	$\frac{18}{100}$	0.18	18%	18
Orange	$\frac{22}{100}$	0.22	22%	22

Wacky Expressions....................................page 35

1. 12/20; 0.6; 60%; 3/5
2. 75/100; 0.75; 75%; 3/4
3. 16/100; 0.16; 16%; 4/25
4. 46/200; 0.23; 23%; 23/100
5. 85/100; 0.85; 85%; 17/20
6. 4/100; 0.04; 4%; 1/25

Presto Chango! ....page 36

1. 0.45	2. 0.75	3. 111%	4. 53%
5. 310%	6. 0.25	7. 262%	8. 0.14
9. 0.44	10. 0.01	11. 532%	12. 5.55
13. <	14. >	15. <	16. <
17. >	18. <	19. 10%	20. 0.8

Fishing Out Percents ....page 37

1. 15	2. 69	3. 162	4. 16
5. 54	6. 6	7. 4	8. 96
9. 36	10. 45	11. 30	12. 14
13. 12	14. 559	15. $376.56	

Running Around in Circles ....page 38

Answers may vary slightly.

1. A = 17%, B = 25%, C = 8%, D = 17%, E = 33%
2. A = 25%, B = 17%, C = 25%, D = 25%, E = 8%
3. A = 33%, B = 33%, C = 17%, D = 17%
4. A = 17%, B = 17%, C = 17%, D = 17%, E = 16%, F = 8%, G = 8%
5. A. 50%, B. 12%, C. 13%, D. 25%
6. A. 12%, B. 25%, C. 13%, D. 50%

Drive Away with Percents! ....page 39

1. 24	2. 7.2	3. $4,000
4. $3,000	5. $36.00	6. 33%
7. 33%	8. 40	

Way Out Ratios ....page 40

Answer order may vary.

1. 5 to 1	2. 5/1	3. 5 : 1
4. 68/17	5. 68 : 17	6. 68 to 17
7. 25 : 11	8. 25 to 11	9. 25/11
10. 10 to 13	11. 10/13	12. 10:13
13. 4/9	14. 4 : 9	15. 4 to 9
16. 7 : 1	17. 7 to 1	18. 7/1
19. 27/13	20. 27:13	21. 27 to 13
22. 51 : 16	23. 51 to 16	24. 51/16
25. 30 to 4	26. 30/4	27. 30 : 4
28. 47/20	29. 47 : 20	30. 47 to 20
31. 21 : 5	32. 21 to 5	33. 21/5

Be a Sport! ....

1. 6 to 9; 6 : 9; 6/9
2. 6 to 6; 6 : 6; 6/6
3. 6 to 16; 6 : 16; 6/16
4. 9 to 6; 9 : 6; 9/6
5. 16 to 6; 16 : 6; 16/
6. soccer to footb
7. soccer, beach
8. hockey puck

Food Fun......................................

E. 4 to 11; 4 : 11; 4/11	T. 7 to 5; 7 :
A. 6 to 4; 6 : 4; 6/4	O. 5 to 11; 5 : 11; 5/11
H. 7 to 6; 7 : 6; 7/6	E. 11 to 6; 11 : 6; 11/6
L. 7 to 4; 7 : 4; 7/4	F. 4 to 5; 4 : 5; 4/5
H. 4 to 6; 4 : 6; 4/6	T. 5 to 6; 5 : 6; 5/6
R. 11 to 4; 11 : 4; 11/4	H. 5 to 7; 5 : 7; 5/7

The Other Half

Cookie Caper ....page 43

1. 4 1/2, 2, 1 1/3, 2, 2/3, 2, 2, 4
2. 3, 1 1/3, 8/9, 1 1/3, 4/9, 1 1/3, 1 1/3, 2 2/3
3. 2 13/16, 1 1/4, 5/6, 1 1/4, 5/12, 1 1/4, 1 1/4, 2 1/2
4. 5 5/6, 2 1/2, 1 2/3, 2 1/2, 5/6, 2 1/2, 2 1/2, 5

Clean Out That Closet! ....page 44

Socks

1	3	1/3	1 : 3
2	6	2/6	2 : 6
3	9	3/9	3 : 9
4	12	4/12	4 : 12
5	15	5/15	5 : 15

Clothes

2	5	2/5	2 : 5
4	10	4/10	4 : 10
8	20	8/20	8 : 20
16	40	16/40	16 : 40
32	80	32/80	32 : 80

Shoes

1	6	1/6	1 : 6
2	12	2/12	2 : 12
3	18	3/18	3 : 18
4	24	4/24	4 : 24

Toys

3	4	3/4	3 : 4
6	8	6/8	6 : 8
12	16	12/16	12 : 16
24	32	24/32	24 : 32

	2	½	3	1	¾
	4	¾	6	2	½
	6	1⅖	9	3	⅔
16	8	1⅛	12	4	1¾
20	10	2⁰⁄₁₀	15	5	1⅗
24	12	2⁴⁄₁₂	18	6	1⅚
28	14	2⁸⁄₁₄	21	7	2½

Setting Up Shop ....page 46
1. $149.50 2. $4.51 3. $1.22 4. $23.49
5. $5.87

Candy Store Story Problems ....page 47
1. $54.40 2. $30.00 3. $1,447.16
4. $55.00 5. $72.90 6. $65.00
7. $466.29 8. $45.77 9. 16 bags; $8.00

Two-Stepping ....page 48
1. $2.35 2. $3.45 3. $2.00 4. 8,904
5. $0.06 6. hamburgers—232
7. candy corn—$1.34 more

No Problem Story Problems ....page 49
1. She sold 632 doughnuts. Each doughnut costs $0.30.
2. 102 left
3. 510 boxes
4. 250 pies; she earned $1,184.75.
5. 16 red; 17 students did not get yellow.
6. 69 women
7. 234 quarts; $535.86 earned
8. 63 red; 28 yellow

Hanging Out with Mental Math ....page 50
Answers are approximations.
1. $39.00; no 2. $9.00 3. $90.00
4. $2.50 5. 300 6. $36,000

Review of Story Problems ....page 51
1. 846
2. 527 fell over
3. 7 groups
4. 210 hours; 45 more hours
5. 12¢ each
6. ham and cheese subs; 24 more toppings
7. 72
8. 244 quarts; $117.60 more

Make Cents? ....page 52
1. yes
2. no; 15% of $180 is $27 and $180 minus $27 is $153.00.
3. no; the membership increased 60% but decreased 37.5%.
4. yes
5. yes

Factoring Out ....page 53
1. 2, 2, 5, 5 2. 2, 2, 3, 7 3. 2, 2, 3, 3
4. 2, 2, 2, 3 5. 2, 3, 3, 3 6. 2, 3, 11
7. 2, 2, 23 8. 2, 3, 13

Bubble Trouble ....page 54
1. GCF = 4 2. GCF = 6
3. GCF = 12 4. GCF = 2

Exciting Exponents ....page 55
Across
1. forty 2. fourteen 3. eleven
Down
1. fifty 2. four 3. sixty
4. three 5. one

Multiply Out ....page 56
1. 80, 20, 120, 40, 60 2. 25, 100, 50, 75
3. 12, 96, 36, 84, 24, 60 4. 80, 20, 120, 40, 60
5. 80, 8, 120, 16, 72, 88, 96
6. 16, 96, 32, 48, 64 7. 14, 56, 28, 70, 84, 42
8. 88, 11, 55, 22, 99 9. 90, 30, 120, 60
10. $y = 28$ 11. $b = 72$
12. $c = 23$ 13. $h = 15$
14. $i = 5$ 15. $x = 9$
16. $p = 16$ 17. $m = 100$

What's the Pattern? ....page 57
Answers will vary. Possible answers are:
1. A number divided by itself equals 1.
2. a. A number plus a number is equal to the sum of the numbers.
   b. $a + b = b + a$
3. a. A kilometer is equal to 1,000 meters.
   b. $a = 1,000b$

Penny Counter ....page 58
From left to right, top to bottom: 874; 466; 867; 473; 1,340; 114; 918; 536; 1,454; 149; 1,032; 571; 1,603
Total: 6,000
Average: about 857 pennies

What Do You Mean by Median? ....page 59
1. $(9 + 5 + 7 + 8 + 11) \div 5 = $ mean
2. 8
3. 8
4. $(17 + 15 + 11 + 14 + 9 + 6 + 21 + 6 + 9) \div 9 = $ mean
5. 12
6. 11

Numerical Expressions........................page 60
1. $9 \times 9 = 81$
   $2 \times 24 = 48$
   $81 - 48 = 33$
2. $100 \div 5 = 20$
   $20 \times 3 = 60$
3. $4 \times 11 = 44$
   $6 \times 2 = 12$
   $44 - 12 = 32$
4. $2 \times 2 = 4$
   $3.478 \times 4 = 13.912$
5. division
6. power
7. addition
8. multiplication
9. 262,169
10. 1,060

Order Up! ....page 61
1. 91
2. 30
3. 42
4. −11
5. 74
6. −10
7. −66
8. 9

Writing Algebraic Expressions ....page 62
1. $a - 5$
2. $6a + 7a$
3. $\frac{2}{3}b - 11$
4. $10 + (c \div 3)$
5. $9d - 7$
6. a number minus 4, times 2
7. 2 plus 6 times a number
8. a number plus 12 and multiplied by 3
9. a number to the fifth power
10. 4 times 5, plus a number
11. Answers will vary.

Express It ....page 63
Answers may vary.
1. a number minus 6
2. a number divided by 5
3. the product of 3 numbers
4. the sum of a number and $\frac{5}{10}$
5. 24 decreased by a number
6. 2 times a number, increased by 3
7. add, plus, and
8. multiply, times, by
9. divide
10. subtract, minus, less
11. equal, same as
12. divide, into

Simplifying Expressions ....page 64
1. $-7a + -7b$
2. $xy - 4x$
3. $-\frac{2}{3}c - -80$
4. $-4t + -48$
5. $3a + 5b$
6. $-10 - 18x$
7. $55m + 63$
8. $-54x - 18$

Solving ....page 65
1. $a = 15$
2. $b = 28$
3. $m = 11.62$
4. $y = 14.3$
5. $m = -1.3$
6. $p = 1\frac{1}{5}$
7. $x = 33$
8. $a = -14$

It Varies...............................page 66
1. $a = 11$
2. $x = 0.5$
3. $b = \frac{1}{4}$
4. $a = -\frac{1}{3}$
5. $a = 364$
6. $u = 56$
7. $x = 245$
8. $n = -1$
9. $x = 36$
10. $y = 0.0144$
11. $3a = 135$; $135 \div 3 = a$; 45 students
12. $2m = s$; $s \div m = 2$
    (Students may find it valuable to match the variable to the missing information. For example, m = members; s = snacks.)

Amazing Algebra ....page 67
1. $a = 51$
2. $g = 372$
3. $b = 221$
4. $h = 1,159$
5. $c = 414$
6. $i = 7$
7. $d = 272$
8. $j = 30$
9. $e = 24$
10. $k = 1,174$

Expressive Equations ....page 68
1. $a = 9$; $b = 6$; $c = 3$
2. $h = 6$; $g = 2$; $e = 8$; $f = 4$; $d = 24$
3. $J = 4$; $I = 10$; $K = 20$; $L = 5$
4. $n = 12$; $o = 4$; $p = 2$; $m = 8$
5. $q = 0$; $r = 4$; $s = 6$; $t = 5$; $u = 2$

What If? ....page 69
1. 79; 162; 157
2. 12; 6; 8
3. 6; 32; 448
4. 84; 88.3; 123 ½
5. 7; 90.5; ⅟₂₅
6. 192.5; 45,472; 147,840
7. a. 300 sq. ft.
   b. 630.75 sq. ft.
   c. 99.1875 sq. ft.

Expressing Ourselves ....page 70
1. a. −2
   b. −50
2. a. 48
   b. 96
3. a. 28
   b. 12
4. a. −12
   b. 22
   c. 46,656
5. a. 24
   b. 4
   c. 80

Evaluating Expressions ....page 71
1. −2
2. 8
3. 40
4. 26
5. 4
6. −88

Mixed Practice ....page 72
1. x = ⁻4   2. w = 71   3. y = ⁻12
4. m = ⅙   5. m = ⁻4   6. x = 1/128
7. y = 0.9   8. y = ⁻22   9. r = ⁻20
10. x = 0

Shapes Face Off ....page 73
1. congruent   2. congruent
3. congruent   4. similar
5. congruent   6. similar
7. congruent   8. similar
9. congruent   10. similar
11. similar   12. congruent

Similar Sensation ....page 74
1. 2   2. ½   3. 10   4. 4
5. 2   6. 3   7. 3   8. 4
9. 15   10. 1

Mirror Image ....page 75

B, K, E, W, H, O
BOX   COOK   KICK

Points, Lines, and Planes..........................page 76
1. true   2. false
3. true   4. true
5. true   6. false
7. true   8. false
9. false   10. false
11. collinear; coplanar
12. noncollinear; coplanar
13. noncollinear; noncoplanar
14. noncollinear; coplanar
15. noncollinear; noncoplanar
16. noncollinear; noncoplanar

Plotting Points...page 77
1. 6 sides; 6 vertices
2. Answers will vary.
3. congruent
4. Answers will vary: two rhombuses; 4 trapezoids; or one rectangle and four triangles.

Ship Shape ....page 78

Puzzling Perimeters ....page 79
1. 48 feet   2. 16 sections   3. $63.20
4. 32 feet   5. 24 feet   6. 11 sections

Size It Up ....page 80
1. 16 m   2. 74 m   3. 16 m   4. 27 m
5. 35 m   6. 23 m   7. 25 m   8. 35 m

Is It Right? ....page 81
Shaded problems: 1, 3, 5, 6, 7
2. 155 cm²   4. 60 m²
8. 40 mm²

What's My Angle?...page 82
A = 40°   B = 63°   C = 64°   D = 95°
E = 60°   F = 71°   G = 57°   H = 40°
I = 75°   J = 139°   K = 67°   L = 14°
M = 71°
Obtuse: 2   Acute: 4   Right: 7

Sail Away with Angles................................page 83
1. 21°—right   2. 126°—obtuse
3. 98°—obtuse   4. 47°—acute
5. 74°—acute   6. 58°—acute
7. 63°—right   8. 37°—acute
Seagulls

Triangles ....page 84
1. acute   2. right
3. equiangular   4. obtuse
5. a. PAR, CMH
   b. PAR, MCH
   c. RCH, AMH, MPC

Exploring Circumference and Diameter ....page 85
1. CD   2. AB   3. EF   4. 90°
5. 7 feet
6. 2.5 feet
7. 648 inches
8. 2 feet 9 inches

Diameter v. Circumference...............page 86

11 cm	34.5 cm	$^{34.5}/_{11}$	3.14
2.8 cm	8.8 cm	$^{8.8}/_{2.8}$	3.14
6 cm	18.8 cm	$^{18.8}/_{6}$	3.14
15 cm	47.1 cm	$^{47.1}/_{15}$	3.14
8 cm	25.1 cm	$^{25.1}/_{8}$	3.14
9 cm	28.3 cm	$^{28.3}/_{9}$	3.14
12 cm	37.7 cm	$^{37.7}/_{12}$	3.14
3 cm	9.4 cm	$^{9.4}/_{3}$	3.14
4 cm	12.6 cm	$^{12.6}/_{4}$	3.14
5 cm	15.7 cm	$^{15.7}/_{5}$	3.14

Concept Review of Circles ....page 87

1. 30 in.
2. circumference
3. 30 in.
4. $\overline{EF}$
5. 15 in.
6. 90°

16 cm	50.2 cm	$^{50.2}/_{16}$	3.14	8 cm
15.5 cm	48.6 cm	$^{48.6}/_{15.5}$	3.14	7.75 cm
9 cm	28.3 cm	$^{28.3}/_{9}$	3.14	4.5 cm
6 cm	18.8 cm	$^{18.8}/_{6}$	3.14	3 cm
8 cm	25.1 cm	$^{25.1}/_{8}$	3.14	4 cm
10 cm	31.4 cm	$^{31.4}/_{10}$	3.14	5 cm

Area ....page 88

1. 15 square units
2. 28 square units
3. 24 square units
4. 24 square units
5. 10 square units
6. 15 square units
7. 45 square units
8. 20 square units

Fill Me Up ....page 89

1. 840 m³
2. 324 m³
3. 5,082 m³
4. 105 m³
5. 2,400 m³
6. 54 m³
7. 54 m³
8. 105 m³
9. 324 m³
10. 840 m³ **Total:** 10,128 m³

Prisms...............page 90

1. 64 cubic units
2. 12 cubic units
3. 544 cubic units
4. 30 cubic units
5. 160 cubic units
6. 75 cubic units
7. 24 cubic units
8. 27 cubic units

Conversions ....page 91

1. 8 yd.
2. 84 in.
3. 8 ft.
4. 240 in.
5. 9 ft.
6. 144 in.
7. 5 yd.
8. 72 in.
9. 4 yd.
10. 12 ft.
11. 2 ft.
12. 6 yd.
13. 3 ft.
14. #4 won

Popping Puzzler ....page 92

1. 3,360 oz.
2. 4 t.
3. 4 lb.
4. 160,000 oz.
5. 5,616 oz.
6. 30,000 lb.
7. 6 t.
8. 11 lb.

Popcorn tastes even better with butter and salt.

9. ounce
10. ounce
11. pound
12. ton
13. pound
14. ton

Note The Units of Capacity ....page 93

1. 16 c.
2. 6 c.
3. 192 fl. oz.
4. 16 pt.
5. 13.5 pt.
6. 20 pt.
7. 28 pt.
8. 12 qt.
9. 12 qt.
10. =
11. =
12. <
13. >
14. >
15. <

It's Hot and Cold Outside ....page 94

1. 5° F
2. −7° F
3. 32°F
4. 20° F
5. 98.6° F
6. 212° F
7. 93° F
8. 98° F
9. 1, 2, 4
10. 180° F
11. 114° F
12. 39° F
13. 5.6° F

Measuring Metrics ....page 95

1. 4,000 cm
2. 16,000 mm
3. 24 m
4. 60,000 mm
5. 3,200 cm
6. 700 cm
7. 5,000 mm
8. 12,000 mm
9. 2,000 mm
10. 10 mm
11. 2 cm
12. 5 m
13. 250 cm
14. 0.15 m
15. 20 mm
16. 400 cm
17. Kiri's
18. Kiri's

Here's a Challenge for You ....page 96

1. 4 loaves; 1 meter
2. 4 bricks
3. yes; 18 chairs
4. 7 meters
5. They will have 20 cm more than 1 meter remaining.

On the Move with Metric Units ....page 97

1. kg
2. g
3. kg
4. mg
5. mg
6. kg
7. kg
8. g
9. kg
10. kg
11. kg
12. 2,000 mg
13. 3 kg
14. 25 kg
15. 5 t
16. 6,000 kg
17. 2,000 g
18. 4,500 kg
19. 36 kg

Rotational Rhetoric ....page 98

It is rotating at one thousand miles per hour!

Unbelievable Units of Capacity ....page 99

1. 900 L   2. 250 mL
3. 4 L   4. 100 L
5. 1 L   6. 20 L
Metric
7. L   8. mL
9. L   10. L
11. L

Crossword Conversions...................................page 100

Across	Down
1. thirteen	1. ten
3. eleven	2. zero
4. fourteen	4. four
7. two	5. twelve
8. thirty	6. nine
9. eight	8. twenty-five
11. five	10. twenty
12. seven	11. fifty
14. three	12. six
15. eighty	13. one
17. ninety	16. thirty-two

Sensational Celsius ....page 101

1. 0° C
2. 37.5° C
3. 100° C
4. 4 ° C

5.
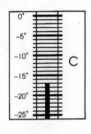

6.
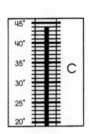

7.
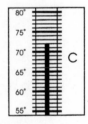

8.
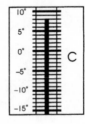

9. 62.5° C
10. 100° C; 212° F
11. 4° C
12. 0° C; 32° F

Calculator Conversions ....page 102

1. 4.8 km   2. 8 km
3. 16 km   4. 3.2 km
5. 9.6 km   6. 6.4 km
7. 14.4 km   8. 11.2 km
9. 19.2 km   10. 40 km
11. 24 km   12. 12.8 km
13. 1.6 km   14. 0.8 km

How Do They Compare? ....page 103

1. 5.5 kg   2. 2.3 kg   3. 95.5 kg
4. 36.4 kg   5. 11.4 kg   6. 4.5 kg
7. 22.7 kg   8. 1 kg   9. 5 kg

Does It Measure Up? ....page 104

flour—540 mL
white sugar—480 mL
brown sugar—160 mL
vanilla—7.5 mL
baking soda—22.5 mL
butter—360 mL
salt—2.5 mL
eggs—2
chocolate chips—600 mL

A Cold Day ....page 105

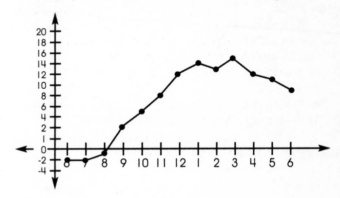

Answers will vary.

The Right Questions ....page 106

Questions will vary but should logically flow from the information given.

Ducky Data ....page 107

1. 8%
2. week 1
3. 145
4. yes; every week two more ducks are tagged.
5. 10; this would be two more than the previous week.

Graph It ....page 108

1.

2.

3.

(Pie chart 1 labeled: Virginia, Mass., N.Y., S.C.)

(Pie chart 2 labeled: paper, cans, glass, plas., rub.)

(Pie chart 3 labeled: deluxe, c/m, ch., c/p)

Double Up ....page 109

1. 5 minutes
2. 15 minutes
3. 35 minutes
4. 30
5. 40
6. yes
7. Mr. Colvin's
8. Mrs. Abed's
9. 138
10. Mrs. Abed's
11. Mr. Colvin's

Comparing Data ....page 110

1. 8 million
2. 1 million
3. 5 million
4. 1 million
5. State A
6. State A; 1.5 million

Taking a Survey ....page 111

1. Answers will vary.
2. Answers will vary.
3. Answers will vary.
4. 37.7%

Graphs ....page 112

1. Average Number of Rainy Days
2. Number of Days
3. Months
4. September
5. October to November
6. February
7. February; it was the driest month.
8. 20
9. 13.75
10. 10

Family Income ....page 113

1. $5,600
2. yes—3% more
3. food
4. $15,120
5. $1,000
6. $6,600

Finding Averages ....page 114

1. mean: 3.43
   median: 3.29
   mode: 3.24
   range: 0.65
2. mean: 122.43
   median: 111
   mode: 82
   range: 143
3. mean: 99
   median: 100
   mode: 100
   range: 20

What's the Vote? ....page 115

1. Hollyhock, Iris, Daffodil, Black-Eyed Susan, Lavender, Tulip, Daisy
2. Daisy, Tulip, Lavender, Black-Eyed Susan, Daffodil
3. Hollyhock
4. yes; 374 out of 435 students voted.
5. 53.43
6. none
7. 57
8. 77

Diagramming ....page 116

1. a. lasagna, milk
   b. lasagna, soda
   c. casserole, milk
   d. casserole, soda
   e. pizza, milk
   f. pizza, soda
2. a. skirt, shirt
   b. skirt, vest
   c. pants, shirt
   d. pants, vest
   e. shorts, shirt
   f. shorts, vest
3.

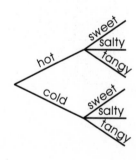

Predicting Outcomes ....page 117
1. n = 16
2. Answers will vary.
3. 96 will pick red.

Playing Games ....page 118
1. a. $\frac{9}{13}$
   b. $\frac{9}{13}$
   c. $\frac{7}{13}$
   d. 1
   e. 0
2. $\frac{3}{6}$
3. Leah—pogo; Leah—yo-yo; Leah—jump rope;
   Shalti—pogo; Shalti—yo-yo; Shalti—jump rope;
   Benny—pogo; Benny—yo-yo; Benny—jump rope
4. 160
5. $\frac{1}{6}$